# *Jamestown* IV
## REDISCOVERY

### William M. Kelso
### Nicholas M. Luccketti
### Beverly A. Straube

The Association for the Preservation
of Virginia Antiquities
1998

# Dedication

To those who, for a century, built bridges to James Fort:

Mary Jeffrey Galt
Samuel Yonge
J.C. Harrington
John L. Cotter
Joel Shiner
Edward B. Jelks
Ivor Noël Hume

Graphics by Jamie E. May
Design and production by Elliott Jordan

Printed in The United States of America

ISBN:  0-917565-06-1

# Preface

*Jamestown Rediscovery IV* is the fourth yearly booklet describing and interpreting the results of the James Fort excavations. As Virginia counts down to the year 2007 and the observance of the 400th anniversary of the founding of Jamestown, it is through these volumes and other media that the Association for the Preservation of Virginia Antiquities (APVA) continues its commitment to research *and* public education.

This work is generously funded by:

The Commonwealth of Virginia
The National Endowment for the Humanities
The National Geographic Society
Branches and members of the Association for the
      Preservation of Virginia Antiquities

*Jamestown Rediscovery* requires a tremendous team effort and I am extremely and continually grateful for the dedicated work of Beverly Straube, curator; Nicholas Luccketti, director of field projects; Elliott Jordan, operations manager and publisher; Jamie May, archaeologist/graphics designer; Eric Deetz, field supervisor; and Michael Lavin, conservator. I am equally grateful to the Board and staff of the APVA, especially Martin Kirwan King, president; Peter Dun Grover, executive director; Elizabeth Kostelny, director of administration and finance; the stalwart Jamestown volunteers coordinated by Judy Corello; and the fund-raising efforts of Mary Ellen Stumpf and Tim Kolly, public relations. Special thanks to our Archaeological Advisory Board: Warren Billings, Dennis Blanton, Jeffrey P. Brain, Cary Carson, Kathleen Deagan, James Deetz, Rex Ellis, Alaric Faulkner, William Fitzhugh, Jon Kukla, David Orr, Oliver L. Perry, Sr., George Stuart, the late Wilcomb E. Washburn, Robert W. Wharton, Camille Hedrick, and Martha Williams; and for the cooperation of Alec Gould, Superintendent of Colonial National Historic Park, and his staff. I am especially grateful for the expertise and generously donated time of Dr. Douglas Owsley of the National Museum of Natural History, Smithsonian Institution, and his staff who have instructed all of us in forensic anthropology. The skillful work of crew members Seth Mallios, Thad Pardue, Danny Schmidt, Camille Hedrick and her students, the selected crew of the USS *George Washington*, and the APVA-University of Virginia Archaeological Field School all made the 1998 summer field season outstanding. Thanks also to the proofreaders: Julie Grover and Ellen, for her unwavering encouragement.

WMK Jamestown, VA 3/27/98

*Figure 1.* The Sentry, *by Carel Fabritius.*

# Chapter 1

## James Fort, August 15, 1607, about midnight

Stephen Calthrop, young gentleman soldier, reluctantly donned his rusting armor. The guardhouse was typically and mercilessly stifling, its solid and windowless clay wall construction yet another miscalculation by the immigrant Englishmen in alien Virginia. Calthrop felt cheated. Although he was a fortunate "gentleman," one of the few men left in the camp healthy enough to shoulder a musket, his reward was guard duty like a common soldier. Yet his good health was a wonder; he was living no better than the guardhouse dog. Eight months out of Norwich had brought him only wormy biscuits, stinging salt marsh mosquitoes, a rotten tent, and, worst of all, no gold. At that instant, the reality of Virginia hit him like a cannon ball—Jamestown was really a death camp, hardly destined to become the gilded city Virginia Company promoters so confidently described. And now he had to go out to be a target for the "savage" Powhatan. More troubling still, he had to watch his back because of his loyalty to Smith, as there was more than one of the President's men out to eliminate the opposition. If only the Canary Island mutiny had worked, he and Smith would have had this place in order! Then he would be free to explore over the mountains and find the gold that must surely be there. Instead, here he was, "imprisoned" in the fort probably to starve to death or

1

die from an arrow wound like poor Brewster did last week. With that dismal thought the sentry cut through the moonlit stagnant night as he begrudgingly made his way to the river platform.

On the other side of the fort, the old soldier left President Wingfield's house with the match on his caliver already burning. He couldn't miss. He had loaded enough scrap lead with the ball to mow down far more than the likes of Stephen Calthrop. The mission would hardly be a challenge for this veteran either. He had spent years in hand-to-hand combat against the Spanish in Holland and lived, unscarred, to tell about it. Yet light from the half moon made his mission tricky; it would give him a better shot, but to be seen out there would be disaster. Mutiny was in the air; the Fort had divided into two camps: the President's men and Captain John Smith's allies. It was urgent that he be rid of Calthrop, one of Smith's staunchest confederates, and be rid of him that night. These thoughts stoked the soldier's resolve as he crept along the town's dusty street. Weaving along the palisade and among the sagging tents and crooked cottages, he approached Calthrop's post. The dim outline of the sentry appeared.

Attonce waited just beyond the forts' bulwark ditch hidden among the tall grass. Fortunately for him, the frail soldiers could no longer keep it cut down. He had been there since sundown hoping his bow would eliminate yet another of these strange English "savages", but he knew that to wipe them out completely would be a mistake. After all, they had "given" him his treasured copper pendant in exchange for mere corn, and with their steel weapons, these men could help his people end the lingering wars with the *maskapow* to the west. But all the same, Attonce's people, the nearby Pasbehegh, had heard that when the billowing sails returned from under the world, more of these English strangers would come to take their world from them. As the night wore on, the half light of the moon made a decisive shot all the more likely. He waited patiently for an unguarded moment. Surely the sentry will walk past a breach in the twisted timber wall.

Calthrop looked out over the river and slapped yet another ravenous mosquito. Dust from the rainless summer burned his lungs and his raging toothache hardly lifted his spirits either. But he could take some solace in his situation. After all, it was still exhilarating to be in this exotic land. Few had dared. And, he reminded himself again, here he had *hope*. He had nothing going for him back home in England, for his older brother stood to inherit all the family land. But with success in Virginia, he had a chance to go back to Norwich with at least some prospect for a gentleman's life. With that thought he turned from the water toward the palisade street. An alarmingly familiar glow of a ready match shone from the shadows just below. His own gun was not even primed! Escape! He leaped to the gun port hoping to drop to safety in the ditch below but the instant he heard the roar, he felt the searing pain in his right calf. Instant numbness. He tried one last time to push through the port but his leg wobbled and collapsed as he fell back onto the platform. Raising his head, he forced himself to look at the mortal wound, and found little left of his lower leg except shattered bone and shredded muscle. He feebly tried to stop the bleeding and cry for help, but he could only manage a weak moan.

Figure 2. Captain John Smith.

Seconds before that, the startled brave saw the sentry struggling through the gun port—a clear bowshot! But just as Attonce would let the arrow fly, he heard the gunshot. Panicked that they somehow saw him through the grass, the warrior turned and ran. He never saw his arrow fly free through the empty port, glance off the cannon barrel, and fall harmlessly broken a hundred yards into the town. Downcast over his failure, the Pasbehegh sniper made his way tree to tree toward his canoe on the Back Creek bank. As he paddled furiously toward home, he wondered if these crude strangers had secret powers to see at night. If they could, he wondered why they had only shot at him once. He never knew the bullet had hit his target. Later he learned that English do shoot each other from behind, to him more proof that they really did come from beneath his world.

The killer retreated frantically back along the palisade street afraid that his pounding heart would give him away. He couldn't be caught out there! Too many men teetered on the fence between Smith and the President. He silently prayed that nobody would spot him and that his hurried shot had quickly and forever silenced Smith's faithful friend. As he heard men rushing toward Calthrop's bulwark, he lurched through the President's door.

Minutes later there was a knock on the President's door. It was the Captain of the Guard.

"Calthrop's been murdered!"

"Murdered?" said Wingfield. "Who?"

"Don't know. We found him dead, bled to death in seconds."

"Hmmm….Sounds like an accident, don't you think, Mr. Percy?

"Accident…yes, of course it was," Percy replied.

"So, **Captain**…it was an **ac-ci-dent** wasn't it?" the President commanded.

There was a long pause as the soldier thought over the situation.

"Yes,…Sir,… a very unfortunate accident it was."

At sunset the next day, a half dozen of the few healthy soldiers left clumsily dropped Calthrop's coffin into the shallow grave not 100 yards from the scene of the crime. The furious Captain John Smith insisted on a formal graveside ceremony. No one noticed Attonce's broken arrow point lying at his feet.

Twenty-six days later, Smith and three other council members had Wingfield removed from the presidency. A year later, Smith, Powhatan's "adopted" son, became President and the colony prospered...that is according to Smith.

Of course, the foregoing Calthrop murder story is a fabrication—total fiction. Or is it?

## James Fort, September 5, 1996, about noon

We found the grave inside the archaeological footprint of James Fort, not 100 yards from the southeast bulwark. Jamie May and Phil Levy soon uncovered the decayed coffin and found that it held a fairly well-preserved skeleton. But they were several hours into the excavation before discovering the lead bullet and severed lower right leg.

The burial was likely as old as the first months of James Fort. It was not only located within the archaeological traces of the wooden palisade but it was also aligned with it. The few fragments of pottery found in the soil that originally covered the coffin all dated to either the years just before English settlement or to 1607-1610. Indeed this was a grave put into

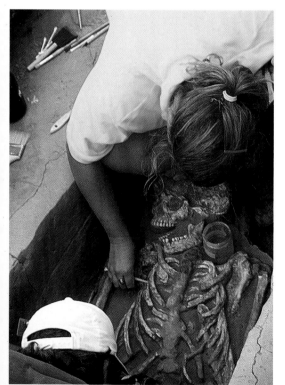

ground that had only been trod by prehistoric Indians or briefly by Europeans sometime very soon after they arrived at Jamestown Island on May 13, 1607.

We rightly guessed that this was the grave of a male, to be confirmed later by specialists based on the shape of the skull and pelvis. The shape of the skull indicated he was a Caucasian, and the fact that this man was buried in a coffin meant he was someone of some social standing.[1] At that time at Jamestown this meant he was likely one of the 54 "gentlemen" listed by Captain John Smith in his series of monographs on the

*Figure 3. Jamie May and Phil Levy in early stages of uncovering burial JR102C, September 1996.*

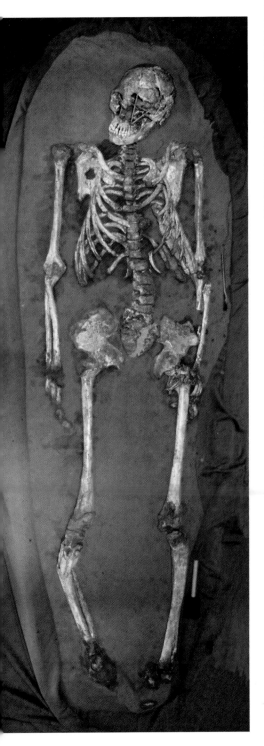

Figure 4. Burial JR102C (left, note broken right leg and bullet) with detail of lower jaw (below) showing serious tooth decay. Objects from the burial shaft fill (above)—broken arrow point, prehistoric pottery (upper right and lower left), early 17th-century Nueva Cadiz bead, and fragment of English Border ware pottery—illustrate the early date of the grave.

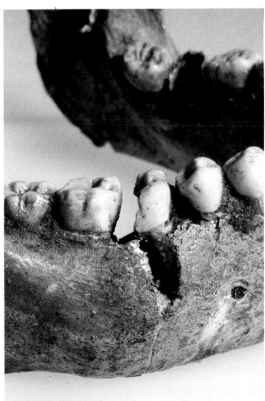

early years at Jamestown.[2] We could also learn from the remains that this person was no younger than nineteen and no more than 22, determined primarily by the stage of development of the wisdom teeth.[3] He also suffered from decayed teeth, one painfully abscessed. Judging from the bone formation where major muscles attach, this individual was moderately muscular but not used to performing hard labor, indeed someone living the life of a gentleman. He was 5'5" tall. We can also know that it is almost certain that he died from a massive gunshot wound to the lower right calf caused by the rear entry of a .60 caliber lead ball and 21 smaller misshapen shot, all of which caused a severe compound fracture of the tibia and fibula. The ball seems to have shattered the inside rear of the lower leg, then proceeded upward along the bone to a point where it came to

*Figure 5. X-ray of JR's lower leg wound showing the lead ball and smaller lead shot still in place, and photo of the same wound area (bottom) with superimposed X-ray shot positions.*

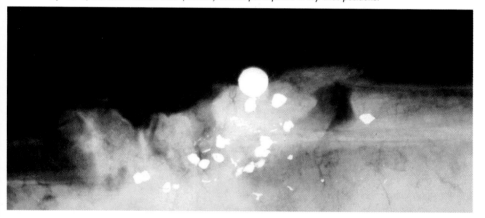

rest beneath the knee cap. The acute angle of the trajectory of the ball indicated that the individual likely was in a position higher in elevation than the gun that fired the shot or that the leg was in a raised running position when it was hit. There was no sign of treatment or any healing; the force and magnitude of the impact of the ball and shot likely severed an artery. Massive blood loss from such a wound would cause death in a matter of minutes. There were no other signs of trauma before death. The fractures in the skull were all caused when the coffin eventually collapsed.[4]

There was a copper straight pin on the left temple and a copper stain, presumably from another pin near the leg wound, suggesting that the victim was either buried wrapped in a shroud held together with pins or wore bandages on the wound and on his head. The position of the legs, spread apart at the knees, seems to indicate that if the corpse was wrapped in a shroud, then it probably came undone when the body shifted in the coffin as it went into the grave. The burial was basically oriented east-west with the head to the west according to Christian beliefs and practices. For frontier Anglo-Protestant Colonial Virginia, this was a first rate burial. Found in the third layer of the 102nd excavation unit dug since the *Jamestown Rediscovery* archaeological project began in April 1994, he became thereafter known by his field record number: JR102C.

# Who was and who shot JR102C, where, with what, and why?

Of course, there is no way to know for sure who JR102C was; there is no grave stone with his name on it. And it is unlikely that "JR" could have shot himself from behind and probably from below.[5] Somebody else fired the gun. However, nearly four centuries after the fact, finding the gunman is as unlikely as learning JR's true identity. Still there are more archaeological and written facts to go on than one might suppose. Like a modern murder investigation, one can string together enough circumstantial evidence to suggest at least the identity of the victim, a possible motive for the shooting, a murder weapon, and a reconstruction of the crime scene.

## The Victim

We can know from archaeological evidence that in or around James Fort, a "gentleman," probably in his early twenties, died of a gunshot wound, shot from a position behind and possibly below during the first months of settlement. From the chronicles of George Percy, one of the first settlers, we can know the names of some of the colonists who died during the summer months of 1607. According to Percy, 24 men, most apparently gentlemen, died by September 1607, after which he himself apparently became too ill to keep up with the death record. No ages are given, but he wrote that Jerome Alicock was an "ancient" (or ensign), which meant he was a junior (or young) officer, and that he died of a "wound" on August 14, 1607.[6] Of course the word "wound" could mean any number of injuries, including one caused by an arrow. However, in a preceding paragraph, Percy points out that on August 10, only four days before Alicock's death, William Bruster (or Brewster) died from a wound "given by the savages."[7] This seems to be saying that an arrow killed Brewster. From that previous entry, it seems unlikely that Percy would not also name the cause of Alicock's wound if it were inflicted by the Indians as

Figure 6. George Percy, author of the most detailed description of the Virginia Company voyage to Virginia and the first five months of the original Jamestown settlement.

well. So why the unqualified word "wound," unless perhaps he knew it was a gunshot wound caused by "friendly" fire. This would hardly be good news to send home, especially by someone who was particularly interested in promoting the expansion of the Virginia Company venture and one who might be urging others to emigrate.

Percy also wrote that Stephen Calthrop (or Galthrop) died the day after Alicock (August 15) with no cause of death specified. This offers the possibility that Percy did not know what killed Calthrop or that he ceased to specifically list causes. In fact, after September 5, he may have felt he covered all the previous unattributed deaths by stating, "…they were destroyed with cruel diseases as swellings, fluxes, burning fevers, and by wars, and some departed suddenly but for the most part they died of mere famine."[8] Percy does not specifically label Calthrop as a "gentlemen," yet other records of him leave no doubt that he was.[9] More importantly there is reason to believe that Calthrop was 22 years old in 1607. A Stephen Calthrop was once a resident of Norwich, Norfolk, and christened in the church of St. Peter Mancroft in 1585.[10] This Stephen Calthrop also had the typical gentleman's incentive to risk the Virginia adventure—he had two older brothers. As third born, he would have been totally left out of any chance of inheriting property in England. In any event, Calthrop is the only "gentleman" for which we have any age data who was possibly as young as JR102C, 22 years old, at the time of his death.

Pure science may offer another insight into the past life of JR102C by determining what he ate. Some of the chemical composition of people's bones is determined by what they ate during their lives. Of particular interest to the analysis of the remains of early American settlers is the relative presence of two types of stable carbon isotopes. The $C^3$ isotope, found in the bones of people who primarily ate wheat, and the $C^4$ isotope, found in the bones of those who primarily ate corn. The bones of fairly recent English immigrants in America, so the theory goes, will show a wheat

*Figure 7. Baptismal record of Stephen Calthrop registered at St. Peter Mancroft, Norwich, England in 1585. This establishes one of the possible reasons that 22-year-old Stephen Calthrop, who died in 1607 at Jamestown, and JR102C, who died at age 19-22, are one and the same.*

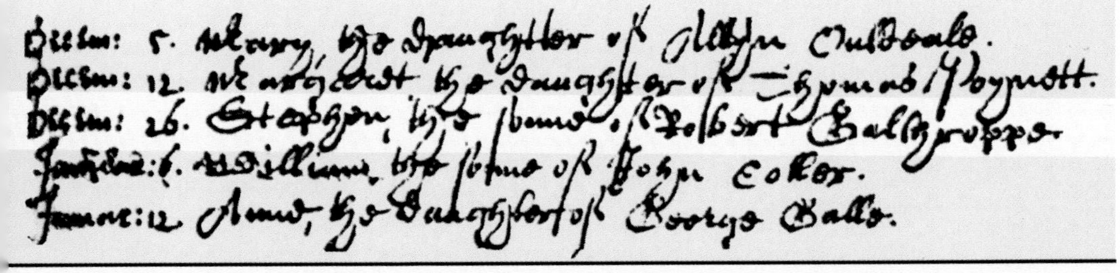

*Decem: 26 (1585) Stephen the sonne of Robert Galthroppe*

*Figure 8.* Summer Harvest *ca. 1615-20 by Bruegel the younger.*

diet, while the bones of Native Americans and seasoned English immigrants would show a corn diet. JR tested out to be very different than either the English or the Indians. The chemical readings seem to be considerably short of the wheat diet and even slightly below the readings for corn.[11] If that test is valid, and the numbers tend to say that something is suspect in this case, then this person either may not have come from Europe or may not have died in the early years of settlement. In other words, if he was European and died in 1607, his profile would be that of a recent immigrant, a wheat eater. He had not lived long enough in Virginia to build up the carbon signs of a corn diet. Or perhaps this man never ate wheat, so he likely did not come from England or Europe either. In that case, JR could be neither Calthrop nor Alicock who both died in that year. Nonetheless, while the tests of a great number of skeletons buried in the Chesapeake region present a very standard pattern suggesting that this procedure is reliable, JR's strange numbers demand other explanation before this evidence can cancel out the documentary and archaeological story.[12]

# The Motive

Science aside, there is more on record of Stephen Calthrop. He was in some way allied with Captain John Smith as they led or conspired to lead an aborted "mutinie" against Captain Christopher Newport and his friends, one being Edward Maria Wingfield, probably in the Canary Islands when the original ships stopped there to resupply.[13] The mutiny must have served to spawn or intensify the distrust Wingfield and his friends had for the commoner, Smith. Calthrop may have gotten off scot-free because he was related to Wingfield, who in turn may have spoken on his behalf to his friend, Newport, and probably to the settler with the highest social rank aboard, George Percy. Consequently, Newport took out his wrath only on Smith, placing him thereafter "in restraint."[14] While this ultimately led to Smith's near execution and exclusion from the first two months on the Virginia governing council, nothing seems to have been done to punish Calthrop. Nevertheless, his part or even leadership against Newport and indirectly Wingfield, who was eventually elected President when the sealed instructions of the Virginia Company were opened in Virginia, certainly must have fostered permanent distrust between Wingfield and Calthrope. As the colony fell on hard times, by August 1607, any animosity among factions in the settlement must have magnified and schemes of mutiny became a logical outcome. Men were dropping like flies that month as disease, bad water, native arrows, and lack of food took their toll. Smith reports only one third of the one hundred and four were left alive by fall. It could be then that the Wingfield camp thought that they would remain in power only if they could somehow eliminate the opposition. So Stephen Calthrop and his mutinous friends may have been marked men. News of political infighting and the assassination of Alicock or Calthrope would hardly be a topic to report back to England, especially if Percy himself was in the middle of it. It is little wonder then that Sir George might underreport the cause of Calthrop's death. Unfortunately, no one left us any more known written information about Calthrop or Alicock or clearer explanation of their deaths.

Although it happened so much later than the JR burial, it is also only fair to mention that there is record of a death, probably at Jamestown, from a gunshot wound in the knee. In 1624, Jamestown's first recorded landowner and Governor's councilor, Richard Stephens, fought a duel with a George Harrison who later died from complications to a slight wound in the knee.[15] Stephens apparently left the field unharmed.[16] In any case, JR102C cannot be Harrison. JR most probably died 17 years before the duel. His wound could hardly be considered slight, and as there was no sign of healing of the bone,there is no reason to conclude that he suffered a lingering death. It is also difficult to explain a shot from behind and possibly below inflicted during a duel unless Stephens could not wait for the ten count and Harrison paced up hill! It is therefore unlikely that JR102C is the unfortunate George Harrison. Stephen Calthrop and perhaps Jerome Alicock remain the strongest candidates for the identity of JR102C.

## The Gunman

Another question to consider about JR102C's demise is if he was Stephen Calthrop and, if Stephen Calthrop was the victim of a political assassination, then was anyone ever brought to justice when his ally Captain John Smith came to power in 1608-09? There is no record of a trial or an execution for such a crime. One execution on record is that of Captain George Kendall who was tried and eventually shot as a alleged spy just after John Ratcliffe, John Smith, and John Martin, led by Gabriel Archer, deposed Wingfield. Ratcliffe then became President.[17] The so-called mutiny is not clearly explained, but there is no reason to believe that Kendall supported Wingfield in any way.

There is some "archaeological" evidence of a gunshot death at early Jamestown that might be suggesting an execution. In 1896, just after grading to stabilize the river shoreline 200' west of the church tower, wave action exposed several human skeletons "lying in regular order."[18] At that time the engineer, Colonel Samuel Yonge, thought these skeletons were originally buried in the early churchyard. He went on to report that "one of the skulls had been perforated by a musket ball and several buckshot, which it still held, suggesting a military execution." Unfortunately he further stated that, "soon after being exposed to the air the skeletons

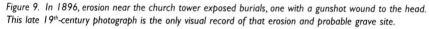

Figure 9. In 1896, erosion near the church tower exposed burials, one with a gunshot wound to the head. This late 19th-century photograph is the only visual record of that erosion and probable grave site.

crumbled." Was this the body of George Kendall? Or was this the body of the man who shot "JR," finally brought to justice after Wingfield was deposed? Of course, without the crucial dating evidence of artifacts from the burial shaft or without the skeleton itself to test for other revealing forensic evidence, there is no chance to learn anymore about this death. Therefore, to suggest that the "1896" skull holding the shot belonged to the killer of JR is pure speculation. In fact, it is also only fair to point out that there are great numbersof capital offenses in early 17th-century English law.

## The Weapon

While it may be impossible to establish *who* shot "JR," it is possible to determine *what* shot him. During the course of the *Jamestown Rediscovery* excavations a number of gun parts were found in deposits that can be dated to the period 1607-1610, all types of weapons capable of shooting the ball and shot found in JR102C's knee wound. The .60 caliber ball, middle-sized shot, and scrap lead found in the bone could have come from a range of weapons, anything from a pistol to a major sized musket. The firing mechanisms from four types of firearms were found archaeologically. These include military issue matchlocks of both the standard trigger and lever trigger types. Also among the recovered parts were a lever-fired matchlock of a smaller and more ornate "civilian"-style caliver and a Scottish pistol with a snaphaunce (flint and steel) firing mechanism. The most common firearm in the collection is the matchlock, a type that

*Figure 10. Soldier firing matchlock musket, the most common type of firearm found so far at James Fort. From the de Gheyn illustrated military manual of 1607.*

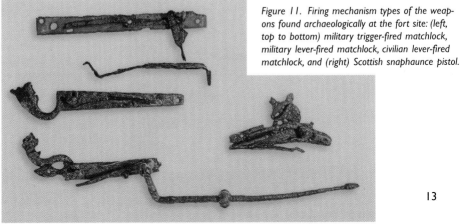

*Figure 11. Firing mechanism types of the weapons found archaeologically at the fort site: (left, top to bottom) military trigger-fired matchlock, military lever-fired matchlock, civilian lever-fired matchlock, and (right) Scottish snaphaunce pistol.*

required the musketeer to light and continuously burn a fibrous wick in order to ignite the powder pan and discharge the piece. This type of weapon would have obvious drawbacks in combat, the most serious being accidental premature explosions during the loading process and the revealing light given off by the match during night battle. A humid and rainy climate, as in a typical Virginia summer, would hardly be matchlock weather either. The muskets may have been loaded from the two types of bandoliers (single-shot powder containers) found with the gun parts or found in deposits dating to the same 1607-1610 period. These bandoliers were leather covered tin or copper cylinders that soldiers carried, in groups of twelve, from belts draped across their chests.

## Ballistics

The 5" spread of the lead in JR102C's leg can be a clue to the distance he was from the gun that shot him. Testing of a caliver and pistol, two of the weapons that could have fired the .60 caliber ball and shot, determined that at point blank range (3' from weapon to target), there is essentially no spread of the projectiles in a load similar to the makeup of lead in JR's wound. This fact tends to eliminate the possibility that JR was the victim of an accidental self-inflicted wound from a dropped pistol. It also eliminates an accidental wound in close ranks. *Someone* fired a gun at JR. The pistol test-fired 8' from the target produced a 5" spread pattern as did the caliver at 15'. These distances and the trajectory of the bullet and shot in JR's leg suggests a number of scenarios to explain JR's death: a case of "friendly fire" occasioned by mistaken identity; a freak accidental discharge in camp; a hunting accident whereby the lead hunter got shot from behind by a stumbling follower; a gunshot wound inflicted by an Indian in a close range battle; or murder among the settlers. All of these scenarios are certainly possible, but other facts seem to suggest that some are *more* possible than others. JR's possible death in August might eliminate the Indians, who likely had not acquired any English guns that soon. The apparent up-sloping path of the bullet may eliminate accidents where both

Figure 12. Fred Scholpp, musketeer at the Jamestown Settlement Museum, test-firing a caliver with load similar to that recovered from JR102C.

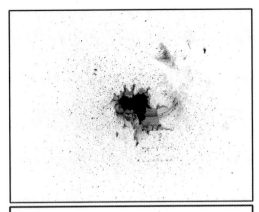

Figure 13. Target shot patterns from ballistic tests: point blank from a pistol (top), 15 feet from a caliver (center), compared with the shot pattern of JR102C's wound (x-ray, bottom).

Figure 14. Types of 17th-century reproduction firearms used in the ballistics tests at Jamestown: matchlock caliver (top) and snaphaunce pistol (bottom).

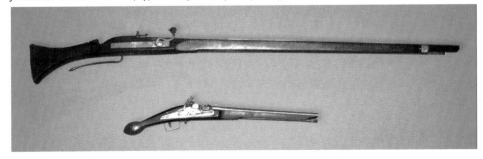

the victim and the gunman were on the same level plane, such as hunting in the flat Tidewater woods. This leaves the freak accident or murder on uneven ground somewhere on the island. The very flat topography of Jamestown Island narrows those possibilities to the following: a shot from the beach up at someone standing on the edge of one of the eroded ridges, a shot from the ground at someone in a tree, or a shot from the ground up toward someone on an elevated position in the fort like the bulwark platform. Again all are possible, but the tree scenario seems remote. If the political motive is behind this death, however, then a bullet shot from below the James Fort cannon platform from a rival's gun is not as complete a fabrication as it may first appear.

## Appearance

A way to identify a modern crime victim from skeletal remains is by reconstructing the face, hoping to find surviving images that match or to find living relatives and friends who could identify the reconstruction. Of course, for a 400-year-old death, identification by friends, living contemporary relatives, and photographs are out of the question. In addition, there are only two known likenesses of any of the original settlers: an engraving by Simon de Passe of Captain John Smith and an anonymous portrait of George Percy. Ironically, they may represent the two quarreling political "parties" at James Fort and therefore may have played some role in "JR's" death, *if* he is Calthrop. Nonetheless, by combining science and art to reconstruct the facial features, it is possible to know what JR102C looked like, in spite of the fact that the skull was seriously damaged in the grave.

*Figure 15. Anthropologist sculptor Sharon Long in early stages of reconstructing the face of JR102C.*

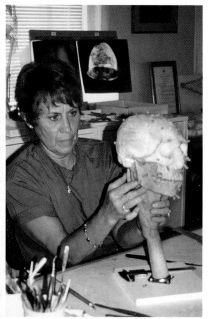

The first step was to reconstruct the skull by piecing together the 102 pieces left of it. That required days of experienced mending.[19] Still the skull offered unusual challenges in that the pressure of the collapsed coffin and soil resting on it caused the skull to warp. The fact that the grave eventually laid below a much traveled automobile road made matters even worse. Add to that the centuries of decay that caused some of the bone to either disappear or become so brittle that it could not be used in the mending process. To overcome that, the gaps in the skull were reconstructed through computer manipulation, electronically "lifting" the unmendable pieces from a photograph of the crushed skull, as it was first found in the grave, and

*Figure 16. Steps in the reconstruction of the face of JR.*

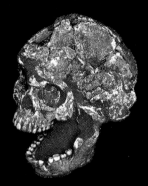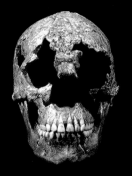

**CRUSHED SKULL IN GROUND**     **SKULL RECONSTRUCTED**     **RECONSTRUCTION COMPLETED ON A COMPUTER IMAGE**

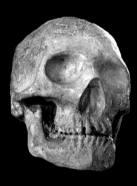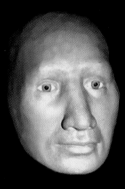

**PLASTER CAST OF SKULL**     **CONNECTING TISSUE DEPTH MARKERS WITH CLAY**     **PARTIALLY COMPLETED FACIAL APPROXIMATION**

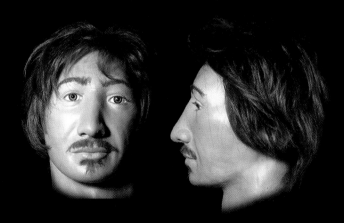

**COMPLETED RECONSTRUCTION OF JAMESTOWN SETTLER**

placing them on a digital photograph of the mended skull. Then parts of the skull that could not be put back physically or digitally were created by copying what did survive on the opposite side, reversing it, and "pasting" it into the gaps. With this mirror imaging, the skull could begin to approach exact pre-death shape.

No matter how accurate the skull reconstruction, it still is, of course, not a likeness of the flesh and blood face. However, the shape and characteristics of a human skull primarily determine what people do "look like" more than most people imagine. Scientifically and artistically rebuilt muscle and tissue thicknesses on a repaired skull can almost bring a face back to life. Guided by scientifically generated thickness markers on a plaster mold of the skull, an experienced forensic sculptor skillfully applied modeling clay to reconstruct JR's face within an estimated 85 percent of its true former appearance. Eye and hair color, facial hair, and hair style are based on examination of 17th-century portraits and engravings. It is interesting that the final rendering of JR looks like a distant cousin to George Percy, whose sharply sloping forehead and rather generous nose match the skeletal evidence of JR102C. In fact, Ensign Jerome Alicock could be Percy's relative as they come from the same town in England.[20]

## The Scene of the Crime

There is archaeological and historical evidence for much of the setting of JR's "murder." The chronicles of 1607, of 1610, and a sketch of 1608 leave little doubt that James Fort was shaped like a triangle and had projecting bulwarks at each of the three corners for mounted cannon.[21] Excavations from 1994 to 1997 uncovered signs of the slot trenches and, in some cases, the decayed or removed side-by-side upright timbers of the south and east fort palisade walls. These walls formed an angle of the triangle at the southeast bulwark, which consisted archaeologically of a circular palisade trench inside an equally semicircular "dry moat" and a number of platform-supporting postholes. Nearby and beginning to form along a palisade "street" was a

Figure 17. Reconstruction of a James Fort "cottage" once standing along the south palisade "street." Signet ring attributed to William Strachey (right).

Figure 18. Excavation site and reconstruction of the southeast corner of James Fort.

series of equally spaced postholes marking the positions where the major support timbers of a crude cottage once stood. Between the building site and the bulwark, excavations uncovered a large backfilled pit. This was eventually filled with trash from the early fort period. The pit also contained clay mixed with marsh reeds, almost certainly the material used to fill in the walls between the posts of the cottage. That "cob" construction is still used in Devon where it forms much needed insulation against the raw English climate. Such construction was not particularly appropriate for the semitropical Virginia summer, however. The settlers finally realized that by 1610, the year William Strachey reports seeing builders at Jamestown abandoning the stifling clay-covered house in favor of the airy bark walls used in the Powhatan lodges. It is possible that Strachey saw the posthole cottage of the modern excavations. As proof he was in the area, his signet ring turned up in the nearby bulwark.

Objects found that were used and thrown away or lost within the palisades are indeed old and military enough to be the signs of James Fort, as well. Excavations uncovered three major artifact deposits directly related to the fort: two backfilled pits and the bulwark "moat." The pits and the moat were all filled at the same time, for the datable artifacts in them all point to the 1607-1610 period. They all contained almost identical artifact types including copper scrap from making trade jewelry, and they all contained fragments of delft pottery vessels that could be glued together from pit to pit and from pit to ditch. All dated coins or tokens found

Figure 19. Stephen Calthrop,
ca. 1607?

in the pits, a total of nine, predated 1603. And the nature of the metal finds from the pits and ditch are exactly the types of things one would expect to find in the fort: a helmet and helmet fragments, a breast-plate, other pieces of body armor, gun parts and equipment, sword and dagger parts, pike heads, powder cartridges, and ammunition ranging from small shot to small cannon balls. Two Dutch political tokens may also attest to the military experience the English soldiers brought with them to Jamestown. Most of the colonists spent years in the Low Countries fighting the Spanish during the late 16th and early 17th centuries.

## English/Native Conflict

It seems that from the beginning, there was little chance that the natives would accept the English whom they felt "were a people come from under the world to take their world from them."[22] War was inevitable. In the early weeks of the 1607 summer, Captain Gabriel Archer reported on native attacks at the fort. One day he counted 40 incoming arrows and the death at the hands of the Indians of "one of our dogges." On four other days he mentions that long grasses and reeds stood along the fort palisades and bulwarks and that the Indians would hide in them and shoot at the colonists. "Sunday [May 30, 1607] they [Indians] came lurking in the thickets and long grasses, and a gentleman one Eustace Clovall unarmed stragling without the fort, shot 6 arrowes into him." Clovell died a week later. Soon after, "3 of the [Indians] had most adventourously stollen under our bulwark and hiden themselves in the long grasses...." Amazingly, it seems the Indians themselves offered a solution to the long-grass sniper problem "He [Indian] counselled us to Cutt Downe the long weedes rounde about our fforte...."[23] Apparently, the Powhatan war policy of attrition was not particularly unanimous. In any case by August 1607, cutting grass must have become a very low priority for the sick and dying men.

Excavations recovered over 100 arrow points inside the footprint of

Figure 20. An Algonquian archer, c. 1585.

Figure 21. Parts of a dog skull recovered from fill in the bulwark trench.

Figure 22. Some of the 84 Late Woodland Period arrow points from across the fort site.

the fort, along the palisades, around and in the bulwark, and in the bulwark ditch. Their shapes and sizes date them primarily into two periods: the Archaic, 8000-1200 B.C. (30%) or to the Late Woodland, 900-1600 A.D. (68%).[24] Likely, the ancient Indians living on or hunting at the Island left the archaic points. The predominant Late Woodland points comprise a unique assortment of shapes, sizes, and stone types together, suggesting that they came from a wide area of coastal Virginia and North Carolina. As many as 30 were found buried with 1607-1610 European artifacts suggesting the possibility that they were being reused by the settlers, who may have adopted the local bows and arrows. Smith reports that in exchange for bells, the Massawomeks gave him "venison, beares flesh, fish, bowes, arrows, clubs, targets, and beares skinnes." But clearly some arrows arrived in the fort during battle. A few of the points may even be from the rain of forty arrows seen flying into the fort by Archer.[25] One broken point came from the fill in JR102C's grave shaft, not 100 yards from the bulwark.

## Environment

Finally, according to astronomical calculations, there was a half moon in the sky at midnight on August 15, 1607, exactly three hours and ten minutes above the western horizon. At that same time Virginia was in the second year of her most serious drought in 500 years.[26] So, August 15, 1607, was a cloudless bright dusty night, and chances are it was unbearably hot and humid.

## "Most feeble wretches" in "miserable distress"

While archaeologists deal with the remnants of dead people and their broken things, they try to picture them as live people using intact things. Speculating about the identity, motive, weapon, and scene of the death of JR is an intriguing exercise, but trying to know who he was, why he was shot, and what shot him is really not entirely why the discovery of this burial is so significant. Rather, going through this exercise brings into clearer focus a number of things about these "able men" in "miserable distress" at early 17th-century Jamestown. As that first summer came to an end, Percy poignantly assessed the desperate state of the James Fort outpost:

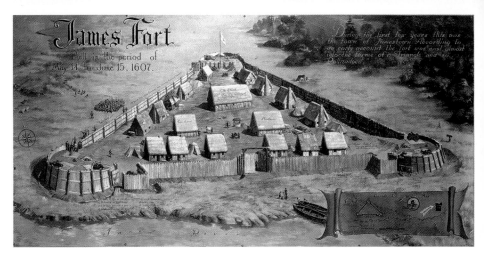

James Fort

Built in the period of
May 14 to June 15, 1607.

During the first few years this was
the town of Jamestown. According to
an early account the fort was cast almost
into the forme of a triangle and so
pallizadoed.

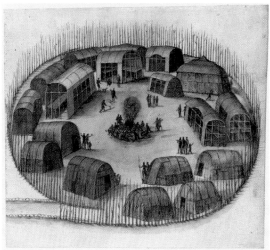

Figure 23. Artist's conception of James Fort based on eyewitness accounts from 1607-1611 (above); eyewitness image of Algonquian fortified village, 1585 (left). These are graphic testimony to the fact that pre-industrial revolution European material culture and the Native American material culture of 17th-century Virginia had much more in common than, unfortunately, either of them realized.

*There were never Englishmen left in a foreign country in such misery as we were in this new discovered Virginia. We watched every three nights, lying on the bare, cold ground...which brought our men to be most feeble wretches. Our food was but a small can of barley, sod in water, to five men a day, our drink, cold water taken out of the river, which was at flood very salt at a low tide full of slime and filth....Thus we lived for the space of five months in this miserable distress, not having five able men to man our bulwarks upon any occasion. If it had not pleased God to have put a terror in the savages' hearts, we had all perished by those wild and cruel pagans, being in that weak estate as we were, our men night and day groaning in every corner of the fort most pitiful to hear."* [27]

In some ways JR represents a typical settler, a gentleman with some military experience, risking life and limb on the chance that he could better his circumstances where things had become "hopeless" back home. It is also instructive to realize that civil unrest must have run rampant at

Jamestown as there was less and less possibility of getting rich quick and more and more possibility of dying young. It is little wonder that the colony picks up momentum as Smith institutes military discipline and a "food for work" program. And finally the Virginia Company starts giving land to those who paid their own transport. Better yet, there emerges something to grow on that land that transformed everyone with even the slightest ounce of ambition practically into instant millionaires. It is tragic that 22-year-old JR, like almost all of Jamestown's original citizens, never lived to share in this tobacco boom. But more tragic and prophetic was the fact that the emigrant English and native Powhatan mostly saw each other as "savages."[28]

## "First Lady"

JR did not lie alone in the southeast corner of the fort for long. Excavations in 1997 uncovered a second burial three feet north of JR's grave, a tiny (4'8" tall) 35-year-old Caucasian woman (field number: JR156C) who died of unknown causes.[29] She was a very worn 35, only five teeth were in place at the time of her death. Some of the rest of her teeth had been missing so long that the tooth sockets had completely closed. The grave was slightly out of line with JR, but basically in the east-west Christian manner. That non-alignment and the greater amount of European artifacts in the backfilling indicated that some period of time passed between the two internments. Nonetheless, the fragmented pottery in the grave shaft still indicated death probably in the period 1607-10. The woman was buried in a relatively well preserved yellow pine coffin.[30] Ironically, while portions of the coffin did survive, the eggshell thin skull was practically the only recoverable bone. Coffin nails survived, and their positions and a ridge of coffin wood down the center of the burial indicated that it had a gabled lid, a common style for the period.

*Figure 24. Burial of 35-year-old woman (JR156C) with surviving coffin wood.*

So who is JR156C? The fact that this burial turns out to be that of a 35-year-old white woman may narrow the possibilities. Women did not come to Jamestown until the second supply, September 1608, when Mistress Forest and her maid, Anne Burras arrived. Anne Burras went on

*Figure 25.* Oderatus by Frederik Bloemaert, born 1610. A mistress and her yound maid outside a watchtower?

to marry John Laydon, a laborer who came to Virginia with the first 104 adventurers, and their first child, Virginia, became the first Anglo-American born at Jamestown.[31] The Laydons were still alive in 1625, when a census lists both John and his wife Anne, then aged 30, and their four children as living at Elizabeth City (modern Hampton) in 1625.[32] Records do not mention Mistress Forest again, which may mean that she did not live long. With so few women in the colony in the first two years, there are good odds that a female buried in a coffin in precious ground inside the fort could well be the wife of the gentleman, Thomas Forest. Being the wife of a gentleman and having a 13 or 14-year-old maid servant in 1608 might also indicate that Mistress Forest was at least in her 30s when she arrived in the colony. Again, with no names and dates on a gravestone, a positive identification of JR156C is as much guesswork as JR himself. But with so few women to chose from, the odds are strong that the identification may be correct. Mistress Forest could be Anglo-America's "first lady" indeed.

Like JR102C, our lady deserves a facial reconstruction. The delicate skull, too fragile to use for molding, makes the effort more challenging. But in this case a computer-generated process known as stereolithography can produce the mold even more accurately than plaster, without as much as touching the original fragile skull. The process begins with a Computed Tomography scan (CT) which produces a three-dimensional file. That information then is transferred to a stereolithography apparatus that

*Figure 26. Fragile skull of JR156C (right) and CT Scan/stereolithographic generated copy (left)—the first stage in facial reconstruction of perhaps the "first lady" at Jamestown.*

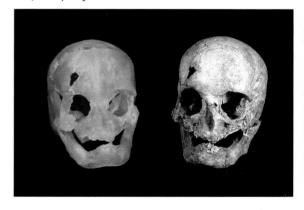

Figure 27. Pocahontas, painting from an engraving by Simon de Passe, 1617, the only known portrait of an early 17th-century female Virginian.

guides a laser beam to exactly recreate the skull in a light-sensitive epoxy material.[33] At that point a forensic sculptor can produce a face through the same casting and reconstructive processes used to recapture JR's appearance. The "first lady's" physical condition at the time of death will not likely produce a pretty face, possibly an image more reflective of the reality of rugged early Jamestown than most want to imagine. Regardless of its final form, in the end, the 1617 engraving of Pocahontas will no longer be the only existing image of an early Jamestown woman.

## Other Graves at Jamestown

In the early 20th century, Miss Mary Jeffrey Galt, one of the original founders of the APVA, lead extensive excavations near the church tower. She traced the brick church foundation, another earlier church inside it, and at the same time, opened some 50 graves.[34] She and others reported some details of many of the burials, including one buried deep with an "Indian arrow head" imbedded in it. They found the stone of what they concluded memorialized a Reverend John Clough and another commemorating a "knight" apparently in brass. While the apparent monumental brass epitaph was missing, the impressions in the stone show distinctive armorial shapes. Found among the two sets of ten burials from separate areas in the chancel, this stone could well commemorate Governor Sir George Yeardley, who died at Jamestown in 1627. Silver thread was recovered from just above the skeleton, but it is not recorded whether or not bones were actually removed. It seems likely that some of the bones generally were left undisturbed and the shafts backfilled, where today they rest beneath a reconstructed brick floor in the 1907 church.

Fortunately, more can be known about burials discovered on the Statehouse Ridge during the National Park Service excavations of 1955 and one accidentally encountered during landscape work near the APVA's Yeardley House. The clearing of the topsoil around the building foundations uncovered the soil stains of approximately 70 grave shafts. NPS archaeologists uncovered the skeletons of ten of these graves and were able to recover bones from six of them. The extremely fragmentary remains became part of the curated collections at the Colonial National Histori-

Figure 28. Mary Jeffrey Galt (left), one of the founders of the Association for the Preservation of Virginia Antiquities, fought to acquire and preserve the site of Jamestown. She also conducted the excavations of the site of Jamestown's early churches and investigated over 50 burials, 1890s-1907.

cal Park, Jamestown. Recent analysis indicated that of the six skeletons that could be reliably studied, there were three males and three females, the women ranging in age from 15-34 and the men 15-29 years old.[35]

While there was too little of the Statehouse Ridge skeletal remains surviving to establish the cause of death, the vast number (archaeologists estimated that there may be as many as 300) and their haphazard alignment strongly suggest that this was literally "boot hill;" the final resting

Figure 29. Archaeological plan of the "Statehouse Ridge" site, showing graves identified during the 1955 excavations.

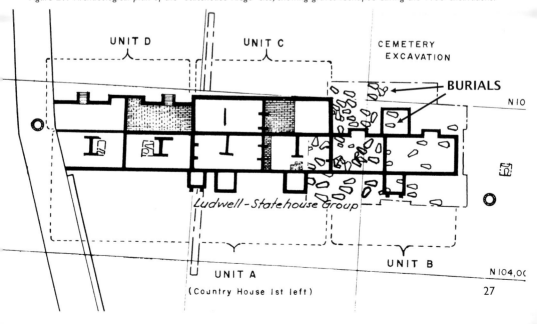

place of the estimated 460 of the 500 settlers who died during the "starving time" winter of 1609-1610. There were so many deaths that winter that there were likely few left alive who were healthy enough to bury the bodies properly.[36] At any rate, the siege of the fort by Powhatan resulted in starvation, probably wiping out most of the settlers in an incredibly short period of time. It is possible, too, that the cause of the mass burials on Statehouse Ridge was not so much the fault of the Indian siege, and therefore the lack of trade in food, but more the result of a widespread problem for both the settlers and Powhatan—drought. A recent study of the growth rings of local cyprus trees old enough to have been alive in the late 16th and early 17th centuries indicates that by 1609, Tidewater Virginia was in the midst of its greatest drought in 500 years.[37] In fact, the pattern of narrow cypress growth rings indicating natural stress could be dated to the period 1606-1613. Therefore, it is little wonder that the Indians withheld food by 1609; they were onto hard times themselves. It also may not be coincidence that the colony begins to succeed after 1613. Of course, that is the same year John Rolfe began successfully growing Caribbean tobacco in Virginia. There is no doubt the cash crop saved the colony, but wetter weather may have given it a boost as well. Certainly there is no additional starving time recorded.

## Risks of "Adventuring Person"

The clear archaeological sign of early death all over the Old Town site underscores the fact that it took enormous courage to come to Jamestown during those first few years. There was danger from every quarter—poisoned water, diseased insects, empty food stores, accidents, warfare with the Powhatan, and, of course, jealousy and political battles within ranks. And after the first few months, it is unlikely that the great risk of an "adventuring person" to the colony was totally unknown back in England. One can only conclude that chances for a better life in Virginia either appeared or actually were more appealing than the real perils of staying at home or risking death in the New World.

# Chapter 2
## Discoveries 1997

### Introduction

By the beginning of the 1997 season, excavations had already uncovered enough of the "footprint" of the timber walls (palisades), corner cannon position (bulwark), and enough related 400-year-old military and domestic objects that it could be said with confidence that the site of James Fort had *not* been lost to river erosion, as most everyone had concluded by 1957. If William Strachey's 1610 eyewitness estimate of the size of the fort is accurate (as it appeared to be, based on what had been found—a triangle of about 1 ¾ acres with perhaps 1 ½ acres surviving), then about 12% of the site had been investigated by the end of the of the 1997 (fourth) excavation season. In fact, for every 10'-square excavation trench opened since the project began in April 1994, there remained nine 10' squares unexplored. There is also the strong possibility that the extension of the palisade found heading east from the fort bulwark is the defense line of "planks and strong posts" erected in 1610, enclosing or re-enclosing the 40 or 50 houses Captain John Smith describes as being there by 1608. If that is true, then there remains an additional two acres to explore in that direction. Clearly there is much more to be uncovered at early "James Town."

Figure 31. Four seasons of excavation have uncovered about 12% of the estimated area encompassed by the original James Fort.

## Goals

The goals of the excavations in 1997 were to: define the estimated shape of the fort, further explore the east palisade line by test excavating a section of it, search for and test the north bulwark guided by William Strachey's decription, and search for the west side of the estimated triangle with a test trench designed to intersect the palisade line inside the Confederate earthwork. At the same time, the areas left unexplored in and around the southeast bulwark needed further investigation, especially to explore the nature and extent of the bulwark ditch and the unexpected "brick" building foundation found to be built over what appeared to be an extension of the bulwark ditch to the east.

## East Palisade

In the previous year's excavations, over 200' of the east palisade slot trench were explored with four excavations at intervals along the projected palisade line. These trenches, except the northernmost, all uncovered the filled-in trench left from what at first appeared to be the decayed palisade wall. Since a section of these tests looked vaguely like the signs of decayed upright timbers in a slot trench found along the south palisade line, it was logical to conclude that the east line held the same evidence. That did not turn out to be exactly true. While the slot trench was there, there was no clear evidence that the upright timbers decayed in place. This became very disturbing, in that while the angle between the east and south wall trenches, 45-46 degrees, exactly fit Strachey's dimensions, without evidence that timbers stood in the trench, it would be hard to prove that this was part of the fort at all. Yet the age and lack of artifacts in the upper reaches of the east wall trench fill strongly suggested that this was an original and early part of the settlement.

Dissection of a section of the palisade slot trench offered an answer to the missing timber mystery. The test trenches near the church determined that unlike all of the other areas excavated in the James Fort vicinity to that point, it had not been plowed. It is logical to assume that plowing near the only visible monument of Jamestown during the later 18th and early 19th century might have been off limits due to the possibility of disturbing graves there. In any case, the real bonus for archaeology offered by uncultivated ground is that there is no disruption of the soil layers from their deposition up to the present. This means that, in theory, the entire depth of the original palisade trench was left undisturbed along some of the east line, offering the possibility of viewing a complete unplowed palisade cross section.

Excavations to that point had uncovered the palisade line from top to bottom, which on the south was logical in that each stain left by the timbers could be removed, forming the earth mold of each post. In fact, that

Figure 32. Overhead view of the James Fort excavation with the cobble building foundation partially uncovered (foreground), backfilled magazine? (center left), bulwark palisade trench (center), bulwark trench (center right) and town palisade trench (far center right), October 1997. Site observation deck is in the middle.

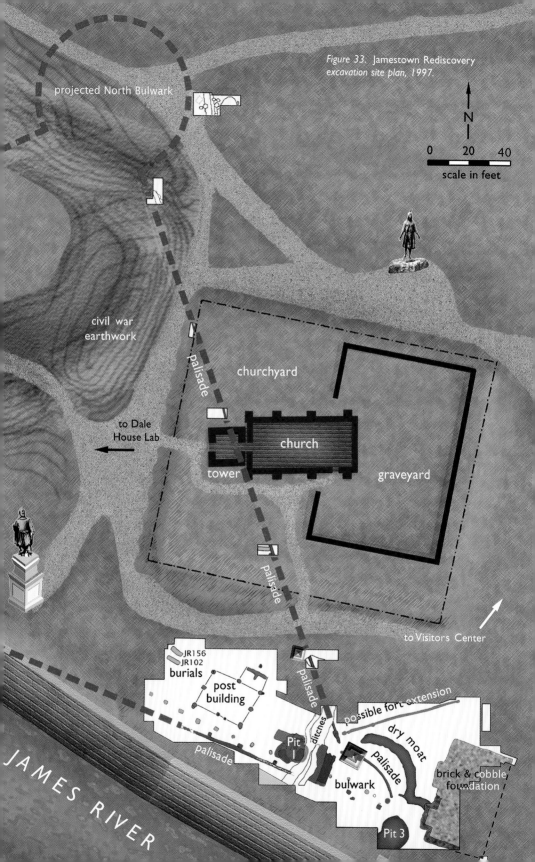

Figure 33. Jamestown Rediscovery excavation site plan, 1997.

N

0    20    40
scale in feet

projected North Bulwark

civil war earthwork

to Dale House Lab

palisade

churchyard

church

tower

graveyard

palisade

to Visitors Center

JR156
JR102
burials

post building

palisade

Pit 1

ditches

possible fort extension

dry moat

palisade

palisade

bulwark

brick & cobble foundation

Pit 3

JAMES RIVER

line was so clear that it was possible, after excavation, to fill the excavated timber cavities with cement and so produce a positive reproduction of the bottoms of the posts. That could not be done on the east line; there were no post stains visible to dig out. So an attempt was made to examine the east line by digging from the side of the trench stain, which had a good chance of revealing each decayed post stain as it was left suspended in the slot fill. Not so. What this exercise did show was that while the original slot trench did indeed once hold timbers upright, they only stood for a relatively short time, after which they were removed by digging around them, then pulling them out of the trench.

A test trench put into the side of the Confederate earthwork along the projected line of the east palisade suggested the same scenario. Only a ditch filled with mixed soil was found in alignment with the other sections of the east line. It was also clear from the nature of the soil layers above the backfilled palisade trench that the Confederate earthwork was constructed from dirt redeposited as the soldiers or slaves dug out the moat next to it. That explained why there were two 17th-century soil layers on top of the palisade slot—one building up soon after the palisade stood there and the other, the redeposited 17th-century town level, first removed and thrown up to the south as the Civil War soldiers began digging the adjacent moat.[38] But why would the settlers dig up and remove the east James Fort wall soon after they constructed it? The answer may come from another archaeological discovery and a closer look at 17th-century eyewitness descriptions of the town's defenses.

## James Town Palisade

Removal of plowed soil north of the southeastern bulwark revealed another palisade running from the east wall line at its southernmost end. This line was found to extend 60' where it came to a gap adjacent to another feature. The testing of the feature identified it as contemporary with the backfilled pits in the fort and the southeastern bulwark ditch. Excavation a few inches below the plowzone along the length of this palisade revealed the clearest stains of rotten upright timbers and perhaps posts and timbers. A 4' section of the line was tested and uncovered the clearest evidence that round sections of trees anchored side by side in 2'-deep trenches was a standard Jamestown palisade construction.

The writings of John Smith, William Strachey, and Ralph Hamor leave little doubt that the triangular James Fort did not encompass all of James Town for long. Their descriptions, read in light of the extended palisade, may also explain both the quick removal of the east fort palisade and the eventual location of the church, directly next to and outside the east wall. After Smith was appointed President (September 10, 1608), he wrote that, "James towne being burnt, we rebuilt it…environed with a palizado of fourteen or fifteene feet…[the overall plan] *reduced* to the form of this ( ) figure [omitted but later called "five-square"]."[39] The word "reduced" is the key to understanding what Smith describes. Today the word clearly means "made smaller," but some uses of the word in the 17th century meant "changed," "restored back" or maybe even "made larger."[40] It must have meant "changed" to Smith, because he reports that by the summer of 1608,

*Figure 35. Town palisade trench showing the soil stains of original decayed palisade posts after removal of plowed soil.*

Jamestown consisted of 40 or 50 houses, far too many structures to fit into Strachey's sub-two-acre triangular fort.[41] It only makes sense to conclude that another palisaded enclosure, probably rectangular in shape, was attached to the original triangle to form a pentagon. This plan offered more than double the space for house construction. Perhaps the palisade trench found extending east from the triangle is Smith's 1608 line, deep enough to support timbers 14 or 15 feet high. A more substantial palisade seems to also be a part of Strachey's description of the line constructed by Sir Thomas Gates and his men after Lord De La War arrived in 1610: "enclosed with a palisade of planks and strong posts, four feet in the ground."[42]

*Figure 36. Removal, from one side, of clay originally tamped around the upright town palisade posts, leaving a perfect soil cast of the base of each side-by-side unhewn timber.*

Figure 37. The town palisade may well eventually define a fort "suburb," not totally unlike that drawn from eyewitness accounts by artist Sydney King in the 1950s.

This probably secured this same housing area in Smith's five-sided town and Hamor's later town that was "reduced into a handsome form [with] two faire rows of houses...newly and strongly impaled."[43] Of course, if the extended eastward line is either Smith's or Strachey's, then attaching it to the triangular fort just north of the southeast bulwark still allowed the bulwark to be defensive. Cannon placed in the protruding bulwark could cover the extended town wall to the east.

These later configurations of the fort palisades may suggest why the east side of the palisade was dismantled. It wound up *inside* the expanded palisaded area and therefore no longer served as a barrier to attacks from outside the compound. It had become obsolete. The expanded palisaded town also explains later church locations on or near the obsolete east fort wall. The church simply kept its position at the center of the new town, i.e. moved from the center of the triangular fort/town to the center of the expanded pentagon. In other words, the church had to be moved east to remain at the hub of the larger community, even to the point that the tower wound up built on top of the abandoned palisade line. This may be suggesting that if the later churches are at the center of the expanded town and the expansion was rectangular, then the expansion to the east resulted in tripling the area of the palisaded town (a total of 4-5 acres). Of course, all but the removal of the palisade and the location of the palisade extension is speculation that can only be confirmed by future excavations along the extension and north into the "suburbs." This is the plan for 1998.

*Figure 38. Test trenching in the area predicted to hold remains of the north bulwark uncovered a complex of early 17th-century trenches and postholes.*

## North Bulwark

The 1997 digging went beyond the Confederate earthwork, guided again by Strachey's dimensions, in search of the north bulwark. There was also anticipation that the north bulwark might be considerably larger and possibly egg-shaped if it was in actuality built as it appeared on the 1608 Zuñiga sketch plan. A trench laid out to intersect what would be a mirror image of the southeast bulwark, (i.e. the bulwark ditch, a curved palisade slot trench, and perhaps a number of platform postholes) uncovered precisely that image. Indeed, the soil stains of what seem to be a ditch, a nearby palisade-like trench and a number of postholes appeared beneath the plowed soil. These features were also found in association with the same 16th-17th-century types of pottery and scrap copper found in the southeast bulwark. But the ditch and the palisade trench presented problems: the ditch was on the wrong (west) side of the palisade and both are heading due north/south and do not curve. Just as it took several seasons of extensive area excavations to uncover enough of the footprint of the southeast bastion to see a pattern to it, so it will require an equally concerted effort to understand the ditches, slots, and postholes to the north. That work must wait pending more excavation in the south extension of the town and the southeastern half of the fort interior (1998 goals).

## West Palisade

Again with Strachey's dimensions as a guide, another test trench needed to be excavated in order to determine the exact location and extent of survival of the west palisade line. By projecting the path of that line from the north bulwark test, a long trench was excavated across a level and tree-free area inside the Confederate earthwork. This determined that the soil inside the fort had been graded during the Civil War-period construction of the earthwork. But the trench did still manage to locate archaeological features deep enough to survive the grading: a sizable rectangular posthole oriented east/west; a narrow and shallow trench about 1' wide and 5" deep; and the edge of a Civil War-period excavation. The 1' trench may be the very bottom of a palisade slot trench. If it is a surviving section of the west wall of the fort, then the angle of the walls at the north bulwark form an 87 degree angle. That angle matches both Strachey's measurements and the 46+ degree angle formed at the southeast bulwark. Time limited further excavation of this trench, and the fact that the Civil War-period grading may have removed most of it leaves identification tentative. Still the chances of finding such a feature on that angle, if it were not the traces of the west palisade line, seem rather slim.

## Pit 3

Excavations of the southeast bulwark uncovered several later features containing second quarter of the 17th-century artifacts, all postdating the occupation of James Fort. These included foundations of a massive building resting on an extension of the bulwark ditch; layers from the building's destruction, occupation and construction; a "landfill;" and sand from what appears to be an in-filling of the shoreline. These backfill layers capped a sizable circular hole dating from the James Fort period, possibly a place to store gunpowder for the ordinance said to have been mounted in the bulwarks. The pit, 7' 6" deep and 15' in diameter, was filled with washed-in clay and a dark organic layer holding scores of artifacts dating to 1610. This collection included a number of gun parts, 1602 Irish pennies, an ornate horse bit, and a medical instrument used to treat constipation. This implement turned out to date the deposit to after 1609, as there was record of it being sent to the colony in that year.[44]

Figure 39. Pit 3, a powder magazine(?), after excavation, Spring 1997.

Figure 40. Ornate horse bit recovered from the fill in Pit 3. Deposited ca. 1610, this becomes the earliest horse hardware yet recovered from Anglo-American sites.

It is clear that Pit 3 was part of the bulwark, in that the bulwark trench was extended in a circular fashion just far enough north and east to allow for the construction of an earthwork along its perimeter. While discovery of the building foundation to the east did not allow tracing the ditch extension beyond a few feet, it is probable that the ditch will continue to curve toward the south to enclose the pit. The extended trench may well be a later addition to the bulwark, possibly part of the renovations Strachey or Hamor suggest in 1610-1611. By the same token, the Zuñiga map of 1608 only shows a circular bulwark on the eastern side of the triangular fort with a rectangular extension to the south. It is possible that the powder magazine, if that is indeed what it was constructed to be, represents part of the improvements made to the fort described by Strachey when he comments that the fort was, "growing…to more perfection."[45] The recovery of the Strachey signet ring in association with the magazine and the fact that he was only in Virginia from 1610-11 strongly suggest the pit is some integral part of the bulwark as well.[46]

## Cobblestone Foundation

The building foundation east of the bulwark was only about one third excavated in 1997. Enough of the building was dug to suggest that it was 54' long and at least 30' wide with two chimneys on the west. The lower footing of the main structure was constructed with water-worn cobbles, perhaps ships' ballast, of a similar nature to the footing found to predate the 1639 brick church. The chimneys were made of brick, the rest of the above-ground building was likely made of timber. Most of the cobbles from the main foundation had been removed. A thick layer of ash inside the bounds of the foundation indicates that the building burned. Some of what appeared to be burned flooring was still visible. No artifacts have yet

Figure 41. Early 17th-century English Border ware bowl from the fill in Pit 3. Its double basins, one made with apparent drain holes in the bottom, establish that this vessel was made for some, as yet unidentified, special purpose.

Figure 42. Cobblestone foundation, brick chimney base, and charred remains of the wooden floor of the post-fort, but pre-1650 building at the southeast bulwark.

been recovered from construction deposits, but the lack of wine bottle glass across the foundation and in the yard area to the west suggest that it was built and burned sometime before 1650. Four postholes and some burned clay within a rectangle formed by their orientation suggest that a shed addition was added to the main structure to the west. A small brick footing and nearby deep postholes on the south suggest additions as well.

While excavations are extremely preliminary, it is tempting to identify this building with some commercial use, such as a storehouse, warehouse, or perhaps a customs house. A 1631 law required an official tobacco warehouse at Jamestown and all trade of imports to Virginia paid for in tobacco had to take place at Jamestown.[47] This would require construction of the warehouse, which may have acted as a customs house as well. Perhaps the cobble work is the foundation of one of those public buildings and may be the footing of the three-gabled building shown on an undated

*Figure 43. Triple-gabled 16th-century customs house, (left) Topsham, England, and detail of Jamestown Island from a Dutch chart drawn after 1617 (bottom). The size and location on the island of the cobblestone foundation at James Fort's southeast bulwark may suggest the triple-gable facade, as shown on the chart, and that it acted as some public building such as a customs or warehouse. Perhaps this was built in accordance with 1630s legislation establishing Jamestown as the sole port of entry for imported goods to be exchanged for tobacco.*

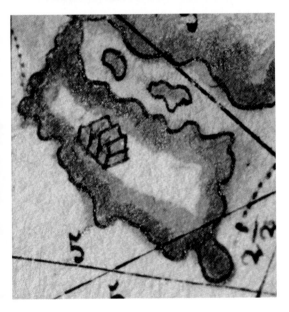

Dutch chart made sometime after c. 1617. It is possible that the Dutch merchants who made the chart were showing exactly where the commercial action was, and that is why they drew similar elevations of multi-gabled buildings at Old Point Comfort and Strawberry Bank at the mouth of the James River. Also it is interesting that the 16th-century customs house at Topsham near Exeter in England has the same three-gabled look.[48]

## Shoreline Erosion

Excavations along the seawall immediately east of Pit 3 in the southeast bulwark uncovered a major deposit of broken domestic pottery, glass, and discarded animal bones—a literal landfill of garbage and trash. The pottery, the types of locally-made tobacco pipes, and especially a Rose farthing of Charles I, issued in 1636-1644, indicate that this refuse deposit is full of artifacts that were thrown away after ca. 1636-40. The material lies under a deposit of scattered broken brick and is capped by a layer of clear river sand which also lies over the burned "warehouse." The brick seems to have come from the destruction of the adjacent warehouse. Since the landfill abutted the west wall, it seems to have accumulated during the life of the building. It is possible that the landfill wound up in that area as a result of an effort by the colonists to build up the shoreline that may have eroded during storms in the early 17th century. Storms may also account for the river sand on top of the landfill and the building foundation. Whatever the reason for the filling, it contained an extensive collection of food remains in the form of discarded animal bones. The considerable quantity of domestic animal bones in the accumulation stand in stark contrast to the earlier fort deposits of wild game and fish.

Just how much shoreline erosion took place in the past 400 years along the churchyard has been the subject of debate resulting in a variety of conflicting opinions. In an attempt to solve that mystery, samples were taken of the river bottom 150' off shore at 75' to 125' intervals. Researchers vibrated 3"-diameter pipes into the riverbed, which recovered a layer-by-layer sample of whatever soil material had accumulated below the river bottom to a depth of 8'. These corings showed that beneath a few inches of relatively recently deposited sand and clam shells, the bottom consists of a 5' deposit of mud above a 2' layer of coarse sand and gravel. Below the sand there appears to be an ancient swamp deposit. Fragments of wood were found a few inches above the lower sand level. Using carbon 14 dating techniques (measuring the amount of the carbon in the sample which deteriorates at a measurable rate through time), it could be determined how long ago this organic material died. The two samples tested turned out to be 2000-2100 years old.[49] The sand layer appears to be the remains of an ancient beach formed as the river washed away the higher dry land at or near river's edge. It is possible then that 150' or less (the distance offshore the coring was made) has been lost to James River erosion south of the fort site during two millennia. But that is only one possible scenario explaining the unusual bottom layers.[50] At any rate, it is clear that because the sand formed a beach 20 centuries ago that is about 8' to 10' below the modern sea level, then it follows that sea level has risen 8'-10' in 2000 years. While more corings and carbon dates need to be analyzed to consider all the possible conclusions that these first carbon dates suggest, the preliminary samples seem to offer yet another reason why the church hill site of James Fort survived the James River erosion.

## Conclusion 1997

The story of early Jamestown continues to become richer with each archaeological season. The 1997 work established that the fort underwent changes in its form and size in the early years, which eyewitness accounts ambiguously suggested. The southeast bulwark was redesigned with perhaps a powder magazine added to it, and the triangular fort lost its east wall as a palisaded "suburban" village may well have been added to the original fortified area. The southeast bastion also experienced storm damage, probably from river wave action, and there was a concerted effort by the Jamestown residents to repair the eroded shore with a landfilling program. Also, coring tests offshore establish the strong possibility that shore erosion near the south churchyard since 1607 may have been minimal. In the same area, the townspeople built a sizable building based on cobble-stones overlapping the remains of the abandoned southeast bastion. This structure may have been built as a result of Jamestown's designation as the sole import port of entry for Virginia. Evidence of the north bulwark survives and appears to indicate a different construction than the bulwark on the southeast. A better understanding of this area must remain unknown until major excavations can move to that area in the future. Additional research suggested the possible identity of a gunshot victim found in the fort in 1996—a 22-year-old gentleman by the name of Stephen Calthrop, who may have been shot to death for his mutinous leanings. That possible scenario and the grave of the 35-year-old woman found accompanying the gentleman's remains serves as a reminder of the very serious danger lurking from every possible quarter in Virginia, the bravery it took to go there in the first place, and the strength of the vision for a better life held by the Englishmen during the early Virginia venture.

*Figure 44. Aerial view of Jamestown Rediscovery site from the west.*

by Nicholas Luccketti
and Beverly Straube

# Chapter 3

## Unknown Soldiers

As a fortified frontier settlement with a paramount need for defense, it is obvious that soldiers played a crucial role in early Jamestown. Certainly the *Lawes Divine, Morall and Martiall* implemented in 1611 by Thomas Gates and Thomas Dale suggest that life at Jamestown was dominated by military decree. Jamestown, nonetheless, was not an overseas military venture, but was sponsored as a business enterprise by a joint-stock company, the Virginia Company of London. Yet, the profusion of artifacts relating to armor and weapons unearthed by *Jamestown Rediscovery* during the past four years gives one the overwhelming sense that early Jamestown was exclusively a military camp. In their glowing account of John Smith after his departure from Virginia in the fall of 1609, Clerk of the Virginia Council Richard Pots and Gentleman William Pettiplace made a de facto "state of the colony" report. They noted that there were more than 490 settlers at Jamestown who were equipped with 24 pieces of ordnance, 300 muskets—including both snaphaunces and "fire locks" or matchlocks—shot, powder, match, cuirasses, pikes, swords, and morions "more than men." In addition to this store of weapons and armor, Pots and Pettiplace state that 100 "well trained and expert soldiers" were present.[51]

Only a few early Jamestown soldiers can be specifically identified. None of the first contingent of 104 colonists listed by John Smith were identified as soldiers, though his roster contained only 82 names.[52] Further, none of the 73 identified colonists in the 120 person First Supply of January 1608 were classified as soldiers, nor were any on the September 1608 Second Supply, when 57 of the 70 new arrivals were named.[53] There are occasional fleeting references to military men at Jamestown elsewhere in the accounts of Smith, Percy, and Strachey. Some were documented only in death, as on August 14, 1607, when "Edward Moris Corporall" and "Jerome Alikock, Ancient," died.[54] Others were incidentally mentioned on various adventures. For example, there were four soldiers among the 14-man crew that accompanied John Smith on his June 2, 1608 exploration of the Chesapeake Bay: Anas Todkill, Robert Small, James Watkins, and John Powell.[55] Both Small and Todkill were original settlers; the former was listed as a carpenter and the latter was unclassified, though possibly also a carpenter. Powell was registered as a tailor on the First Supply, while Watkins, who arrived at the same time, was unclassified, though likely a laborer. Smith made a second cruise to the Chesapeake Bay on July 20, this time escorted by a 12-man party with five soldiers, including Todkill and Watkins.[56] A December 1608 voyage by Smith to Powhatan's home village at Werowicomico on the York River included a barge with six soldiers and Sergeant Edward Pising. Pising was listed as a

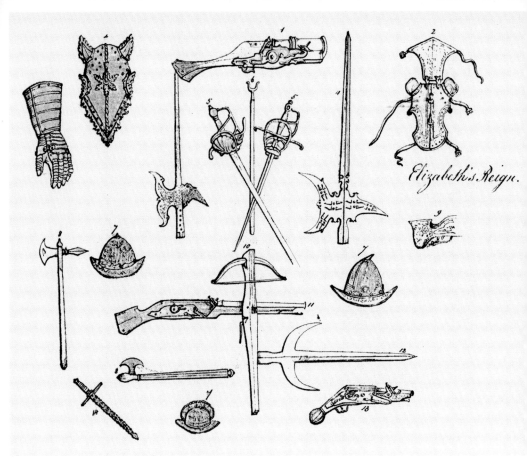

*Figure 45. Some of the arms and armor used during the reign of Queen Elizabeth I.*

carpenter on the original voyage and a soldier on the July trip to the Chesapeake Bay.[57] In 1610 there were four companies at Jamestown totaling at least 200 men; however, most early Jamestown soldiers remain anonymous.

In addition to locating the eastern corner of the first fort, the *Jamestown Rediscovery* excavations have unearthed pikeheads, matchlocks, gun rests, arrowheads, body armor, pieces of bucklers and helmets, sword parts, and more—a wealth of weapons and arms-related artifacts that attest to the pervasiveness and character of the military life at early Jamestown. This evidence provides insights into such questions as: What was the result of infusing a commercial colonial venture with a large dose of military routine? To what degree were the Old World military structure and practices of English armies transferred to a New World frontier settlement and what transformations, if any, were made? How did the controversies in England regarding the modernization of armies with new weapons affect the equipment supplied to Jamestown? And, on a more personal level, what did it mean to be a soldier during the first 10 years or so at Jamestown?

# English Precursors

Although England was engaged in major land conflicts in the Netherlands, Ireland, and France during the late 16th and early 17th centuries, it maintained no standing army as we know it. The military establishment under James I was a continuation of the tradition that evolved during the reigns of Elizabeth and her predecessors. When needed, troops were raised principally from the county militias for service within the homeland, but men were not legally bound for foreign expeditions. An act of Parliament passed in 1558, required all able-bodied men from 16 to 60 to serve in the county militias.[58] The militias were supposed to muster each summer for 7 days of training as well as other times during the year. Since not all militia men were armed or even trained, distinct groups of militia were created, referred to as "trained bands."[59]

The act also designated that a Lord Lieutenant, would be in charge of the militia in each county. The Lord Lieutenants were commissioned to call the musters for training and, if ordered to serve, lead their troops into battle. They also were charged with the disagreeable duty of selecting men from the militias for foreign duty. When a warrant to raise troops was received from the crown, Lord Lieutenants frequently relied on justices of the peace and constables to assist in obtaining the required number of men.[60] In addition to the militia men, volunteers and conscripts were enlisted when necessary and captains sometimes raised their own company for hire. The volunteers not infrequently included the younger sons of noblemen who were called "gentlemen volunteers," and served as both officers and soldiers.[61]

The whole structure of military operations centered around the company, formerly and sometimes still referred to as a "band" or "trained band." In the 1590s, a company serving in Ireland or the Low Countries typically numbered about 150 soldiers, armed principally with firearms and pikes and a small number of halberdiers, billmen, and archers.[62] Companies were under the command of a captain who, in the opinion of many contemporary and modern writers, was the most important officer in the English armies. He was responsible for training his men, as well as distributing their pay and supplies, a situation that lent itself to frequent corruption. The captain also selected the other officers of his company, which in a 150-man company usually included a lieutenant, an ensign, 2 sergeants, 6 corporals, and 2 drummers. The lieutenant was the second in command and was responsible for supervising the troops, posting the guard, and making the rounds. The ensign, also known as ensign-bearer or ancient, was third in command. He carried the company's banner and in battle he was stationed in the center of the formation or, during a charge, at the head of the assault troops. Sergeants were the backbone of the company, deploying troops in battle. They were responsible for drilling and disciplining the troops as well as supervising the distribution of food and supplies. Corporals were placed in charge of the company's squads, usually 20-25 men. They led weapons and tactics training and checked that the soldiers' equipment was sufficient and in proper order. The company communicated by means of its drummers, who carried messages to opponents, beat time for marching soldiers, and sounded commands during battle.[63]

The appointment of favorites as captains, regardless of military experience, caused a plethora of problems. Apart from being incompetent to lead men in battle, many captains' idea of service was to get rich. The most common method of lining their pockets was simply not to pay their men. Many captains did not go on assignments with their troops, especially to the Irish wars. This corruption was so widespread that the word *captain* became synonymous for the word *scoundrel*.[64]

# "Fierie Weapons" vs the "Senora y Reyna de las Armas"

Muskets were used first by the Spanish around 1540 and gradually were incorporated into the English armies; however, this modernization process was a difficult one.[65] During the two decades that preceded the settlement of Jamestown, there was a continuous controversy in English military circles about replacing traditional arms (such as polearms and longbows) with harquebus, caliver, and musket, together called "fierie weapons," by writers and soldiers at the time.[66] And just as there were strong opinions about firearms, there also were ardent discussions when it came to considering the venerable pike, a weapon then still in wide use in Europe and so esteemed by the Spanish armies that they nicknamed it the *Senora y Reyna de las Armas*—the mistress and queen of arms.[67]

## Harquebus, Caliver, and Musket

In the fall of 1609, Captain John Martin was dispatched with a large force of men to the Nansemond River territory and, after an initial successful surprise attack on the Nansemond chief's village, found himself in need of reinforcements. He sent a message to President John Smith requesting "30 good shotte."[68] A year earlier, Captain Christopher Newport traveled to Powhatan's coronation with "50 of his best shot."[69] Neither Newport nor Martin were referring to soldiers that were the best marksmen, since, at that time, the word "shot" was a general term used to designate anyone that carried any type of firearm. The captains were alluding to some other quality—perhaps the bravest or strongest—or to soldiers that could reload the quickest, but not to those with the best aim. The concept of shooting a weapon at a specific target beyond a close range was unthinkable, simply because firearms of the Jamestown period were so inaccurate.

The longstanding debate over the effectiveness of firearms, which centered on their accuracy and rate of fire, peaked in the 1590s with the numerous publications by veteran soldiers discussing the merits of firearms compared to other weapons. For example, the military authors generally agreed that muskets, harquebuses, and calivers could stop an unarmored opponent at 200 yards, but they do not mention how many shots it would take. However, several 18th-century observers commented on the inaccuracy of smoothbore muskets; in one case, it was estimated that at the Battle of Chotusitz in 1742, the Prussians shot 260 bullets for every Austrian soldier killed. This apprehension about the accuracy of firearms was still prevalent in the late 18th century, as evidenced by a French saying that the number of bullets required to kill an enemy soldier was seven times his weight in lead. Although these assertions are likely overstatements, modern ballistics tests definitively have shown the inaccuracy of early firearms. The world renowned Landeszeughaus armory in Graz, Austria, selected 13 muskets and pistols from its vast arsenal of 16th- through 18th-century weapons for testing under controlled conditions at an indoor firing range. The average for mounted and electrically-fired muskets hitting a man-sized target at 100 meters was 50%. The researchers concluded that qual-

Figure 46. English soldiers in 1581 shouldering light matchlock firearms known as harquebuses or calivers.

D

ity weapons outperformed mass-produced firearms; however, inaccuracy was an inherent feature of the smoothbore firearms that could not be predicted and therefore not improved with practice. Thus, the accuracy of poorly made or maintained 16th-century calivers or muskets fired during the stress of combat must have been appalling. Of course, armies recognized this problem and compensated for it by massing soldiers in ranks and files (rows and columns), each rank firing in volley, but not aiming at a specific target. Indeed, this shotgun approach is reflected in the contemporary English infantry command for the movement that preceded the order to fire (or "give fire"), which was "level" rather than "aim."[70]

The 16th and early 17th centuries comprised a time of experimentation with firearms which resulted in many different types and little standardization. Small wonder that references in the early writings to the firearms in military usage at the time of Jamestown's settlement—the harquebus, caliver, and musket—have provided nomenclature that at times is contradictory and confusing. Basically, the three terms appear to refer to different sizes of weapons with the harquebus being the smallest and the musket the largest. Some 16th-century documents, however, apply the different labels to designate firearms with different ignition systems. *Harquebus*, for example, is sometimes used to distinquish a firearm equipped with a wheel lock rather than a matchlock. To set the record straight, Humphrey Barwick, writing in 1594, says that despite what many of his contemporaries think, there is essentially no difference between a harquebus and caliver except that the latter "is of a greater circuite or Bullet" and that its name derived from the French description "peece de Calibre, which is as much as to say, a peece of bigger circute."[71]

The harquebus, also referred to in writings as an arquebus, is so-called from the German *Hakenbüse* or, literally, "hooked gun." This 14th-15th century gun had a hooklike support on the underside of the barrel which would enable it to absorb recoil when fired. By the early 17th century, harquebus was used to refer to a long gun that was light enough to use without a forked support, known as a rest, and thereby favored by the cavalry. A 1625 description of the various strengths required of soldiers to wield the different weapons reflects the characteristically light weight of the harquebus— "the strong tall and best persons to be pikes, the squarest and broadest will be fit to carry muskets and the least and nimblest may be turned to the Harquebush."[72]

The weapon's popularity declined during the first quarter of the 17th century, as the more powerful musket came into more widespread use. But it is still mentioned in the English Council of War's order of 1630 for the standardization of weapons. In this document it is described as having a barrel length of 30", an overall length of 45", and a bore of 17". The caliver in this same order is to have a barrel length of 39" and an overall length of 54" but the same bore as the harquebus.

Whereas the harquebus and caliver were fitted with either matchlock or snaphaunce locks, the musket, with its 48" barrel length, 62" overall length, and bore of 12 was most commonly equipped with a matchlock. The matchlock mechanically holds and operates matchcord for ignition. For over 250 years the matchlock was popular military issue because it was a simple mechanism with few working parts and thereby relatively inexpensive to maintain and repair. A forked rest was required to aim and fire the unwieldy musket, which could weigh as much as 20 pounds, but it continued to be used because it had greater range over the lighter firearms.

The biggest problem common to all matchlock arms, however, surrounded the basic necessity of matchcord. The soldier had to keep the match constantly burning, usually at both ends, so there would be a ready source of fire for ignition. The smoldering match made the soldier, who also had to carry gunpowder on his person, vulnerable to burns from combustion of these materials. In addition, the burning match was a very visible target at night, but was necessary in the face of imminent danger as there was no way to ignite the match quickly. The match could also be easily extinguished by inclement weather, rendering the soldier defenseless. Finally, the matchcord had to be made in England, making the colonists dependent on its supply for fire power.

There are two types of matchlocks, both of which are represented in the Jamestown excavations. The earliest type is the sear lock, which was developed in the mid-15th century, borrowing technology from the crossbow. In this mechanism, the serpentine, holding the burning match, is lowered onto the pan, containing gunpowder, by applying pressure to an L-shaped lever beneath the stock (see figure 11). By 1590, matchlocks were also made using a conventional trigger which was mounted in the stock separately from the lock. This innovation had advantages over the

*Figure 47. Engraving by Jacob de Gheyn from his* Exercise of Arms *of 1607 depicting a musketeer with the standard equipment of the matchlock musket. The matchcord, which must be kept lighted at each end, posed a constant hazard to the soldier who wore gunpowder charges, called a bandolier, slung about his shoulder.*

sear lock in that the lock could be more easily removed from the stock and the trigger could be protected by a guard to prevent accidental firing. The sear lock was probably not made after c.1620 but references to it continue in the literature as old firearms are converted to contain the improved trigger.

The parts to at least 12 matchlocks have been uncovered from features relating to James Fort. Nine of these are of the earlier sear lock type and all but one appear to be of military issue. An intact lock from Pit 3 is finished with zoomorphic terminals on the lockplate and an acorn finial on the sear trigger, suggesting that it is from a civilian arm, probably a caliver, privately owned by one of the gentlemen at Jamestown. Furthermore, there are no gun barrels from the site that would indicate the types of weapons being used.

Since there was little standardization in the manufacture of weapons, as mentioned earlier, it cannot be determined from the lockplates whether they were mounted on calivers or muskets. Examination of the lead shot also does not illuminate the types of weapons being used. The shot ranges in size between 1 mm and 20 mm, with the most numerous measuring in the lower range.

The small shot is also known as birdshot or quail shot and was commonly used for hunting fowl and other small game. Once fired from the gun, the numerous shot would scatter widely, increasing the chances of hitting the mark. According to the documentary record, this spray of shot also was used effectively by the colonists against attacking "Salvages." The early weapons provided minimal accuracy and therefore a scatter of shot, hitting some individuals and scaring the rest, had a greater impact than a single ball shot off the mark. This practice is reflected in an account of 1607, when a group of sixty or seventy Indians armed with "Clubs, Targets, Bowes, and Arrows" charged John Smith and his party of six men. The colonists repelled them with "muskets loaden with Pistoll shot," leaving those who could not flee into the woods "to lay sprauling on the ground."[73]

The larger lead balls, for loading singly into the barrel, range in size from 11 to 20 mm in diameter. The larger of these (18 to 20 mm) were suitable for muskets, but it is not known if the others were being cast for use in muskets, calivers, or pistols. Since, as mentioned before, the caliber on these early weapons was not standardized, the smaller-sized shot could

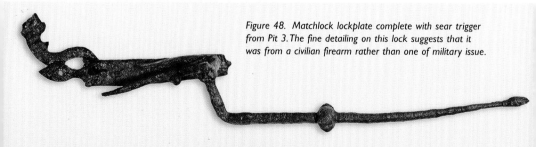

Figure 48. Matchlock lockplate complete with sear trigger from Pit 3. The fine detailing on this lock suggests that it was from a civilian firearm rather than one of military issue.

have been produced to ensure that it would fit down the muzzle of all the weapons in use. Or the smaller diameter balls could have been preferred ammunition just to save lead and/or gunpowder. "Pistoll Bullets" required less than one-third the powder of musket shot, "for alwaies the more lead the lesse pouder, and yet shall the force be never the less."[74]

Figure 49. Assorted sizes of small lead shot that would have been loaded together down the barrel of the firearm for a single charge.

A single pistol equipped with a snaphaunce lock has been recovered from the excavations so far. Characteristics of the lockplate, particularly the jaws which are operated by a screw that enters from below and is secured by a nut above, define it as being Scottish. It appears to be a civilian firearm and was most likely carried by one of the gentlemen of the colony, "for the Scottish pistol was not so much a weapon…but a badge of rank."[75] The snaphaunce lock on the pistol, which was used in England from c.1580, has a flint and steel ignition system. It is "the first form of flint lock to appear on the European scene"[76] and, as such, can be seen as the source for the invention of the French flintlock, whose superior technology was used in most firearms for nearly two centuries.

French gunsmiths took the lead in firearm production in the first half of the 17th century and most of the references to snaphaunce pistols in this time period describe them as French. John Smith recounts using a "French pistoll" against some Indians on one of his forays from Jamestown, "with my pistoll ready bent [cocked]…I was struck with an arrow on the right thigh, but without harme: upon this occasion I espied 2 Indians drawing their bowes, which I prevented in disharging a French pistoll."[77] Later, because he was unwilling to show the Indians the limitations of his weapon, he "broke the cocke" on the pistol to avoid shooting at a target at 6 score (600') that they had set up.[78]

Figure 50. Scottish snaphaunce pistol dating to the late 16th century and which probably belonged to one of Jamestown's gentlemen.

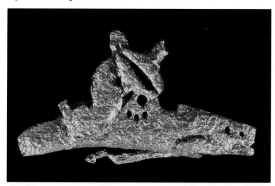

*Figure 51. English soldiers in Ireland in the late 16th century. Note the group of pikemen behind the standard bearer.*

## The Pike

The pike is a polearm of about 16 to 18 feet in length with a small steel-bladed head. At the time of Jamestown's settlement, it was an important weapon of European infantries. It remained so until the mid-17th century when improvements in the accuracy and range of firearms, coupled with the addition of the bayonet to the musket, spelled its demise.

The pike was the most effective defense against the cavalry, and the pikemen who wielded the weapon had a special role in protecting the musketeers while they were reloading. As an offensive weapon, the pike only was efficient in the hands of exceptionally strong soldiers who required the protection of shot.[79]

A helmet, gorget, breastplate with tassets, and backplate completed the arming of the pikeman and made him almost invincible. Pikemen marched in well-drilled squares which, resembling giant hedgehogs bristling with steel quills, presented quite a formidable force to the attacks of the opposing infantry and cavalry alike. When confronting the latter, the pikeman would assume a braced position with the left knee bent forward and the base of the pike supported against his right foot. While the pike was held in the left hand, a sword was wielded in the right. A horseman who drew too near to this prepared position chanced to impale his mount on a pike, which would render him vulnerable to the swinging swords of the infantry.

The composition of the Dutch and English infantry companies, and thus the relative importance of the different positions, can be observed through the yearly muster rolls of the armies. While pikemen formed the bulk of the foot soldiers in the Dutch army and were the highest paid,[80] the Elizabethan armies in Ireland were composed of only 40% pikes, the rest being made up of musketeers and a few halberds. The percentage of pikes diminished even more during the 1595-1601 musters.[81] The same trend is seen in Elizabethan forces sent to the Continent. Sixty percent of English soldiers sent to France in 1589 were armed with pikes, wheras two years later the percentage fell to 40%, and during the first years of the 17th century, the percentages dropped further still.[82]

The pike was not especially useful to the Jamestown soldiers since they were not confronted by cavalry and their principal engagements were skirmishes with the Indians. The pike's effective exercise required hours of drill and organized battle formations where opposing forces formally faced off against one another in set piece engagements. This is not how the Indians chose to conduct their battles, whose "feight [fight] is alway in the wood with bow & arrowes."[83] Pike references in the early Jamestown chronicles are often only to "pike-heads," which indicate that the weapons were supplied in compact form without the long staff, with the intent that the colonists could add these later. There is no mention of the use of pikes by the early Jamestown colonists.

That the pike had been abandoned early on by the colonists as a military weapon can be seen by a colonist's request to the Virginia Company in 1621 for a resupply of the polearm after a perceived Spanish threat.

> ...wee maie haue some Pikes sent vs wch weapon the maner of or peoples fightinge with the natives hath worne quite out of vse but if shall haue to doe wth the Spaniard wee must fight wth him in his treanches wch hee that cann doe with a Pike is a better Soldier then I.[84]

The iron heads to two pikes have been recovered from a c. 1607-1610 context on the site. They both are socketed and have two long iron straps or langets which would have secured them to the long wooden (usually ash) shaft. These straps also served to strengthen the pike in the area were it was most likely to break "if the push be vigorous and the resistance considerable."[85]

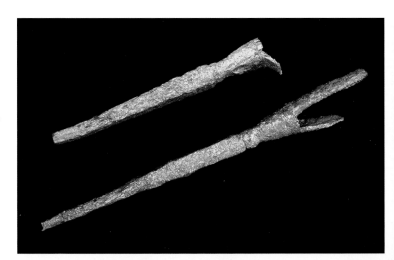

*Figure 52. Two pikeheads from Pit 1.*

The two pikeheads are not of the broad lozenge shape seen in Dutch sources, but instead are four-sided and square sectioned above a decorative knop. Interestingly, all six of the other pikes recovered from Jamestown Island during National Park Service excavations in the 1950s are of the same type. The identical pike type also is represented in the Nova Zembla assemblage from the 1595 wintering over of the Dutch expedition of Willem Barents. There it is being described as a boarding pike, a short staff weapon in use aboard warships from the 16th to the 19th centuries.[86] The narrow blade was fashioned to fit through the grates in the ship's hold so the sailors could defend positions from below deck, as well as offensively probe tight spaces in enemy ships. If the Jamestown pikes are indeed boarding pikes, then perhaps they are not Virginia Company issue but instead represent booty traded by the visiting sailors. John Smith complained about this "underground" three-way trade between the "souldiers," each new shipload of "saylers," and the "Salvages." The sailors sought Indian "Furres, Baskets, Mussaneeks [gray squirrels?], young Beasts, or such like Commodities;" the Indians desired tools ("Axes, chissels, Hows, and Pick-axes") and weapons ("Pike-heads, shot, Powder"); and the colonists, who acted as intermediaries, received payment in the way of "Butter, Cheese, Beefe, Porke, Aqua vitae, Beere, Bisket, Oatmeale and Oyle: and then fayne all ws sent them from their friends."[87]

## "Unfitt for any Moderne Service"

For much of the 16th century, soldiers and mercenary bands were equipped with arms that had been used for generations. The principal weapons of medieval English armies were the renowned longbow and "brown bill," which were heavily challenged by the increasing development and use of firearms. Military archery, along with the men skilled in its use, dwindled toward the end of the 16th century. In a 1585 document advising Sir Walter Raleigh on the ideal military component for a colony, it was suggested that of 800 soldiers, 400 were to be armed with firearms with only 150 to carry the longbow. The remaining 250 men would be equipped with short weapons, swords, and targets or shields.[88] Ten years later, the English Privy Council ordered that archers should no longer be recruited into companies, and they soon disappeared completely from the militia muster rolls.[89]

Just as the longbow succumbed to the march of progress, so did the bill and halberd, also known as polearms or staff weapons. Bills, like longbows, were still used in large numbers as late as 1584, when a 7400-man English infantry on the Scottish border had 2500 billmen.[90] As late as 1601, an act of the Privy Council instructed that a company of 100 soldiers should have 12 billmen.[91] But for the most part, the bill lost its value by the time the colonists first set foot on Jamestown Island.

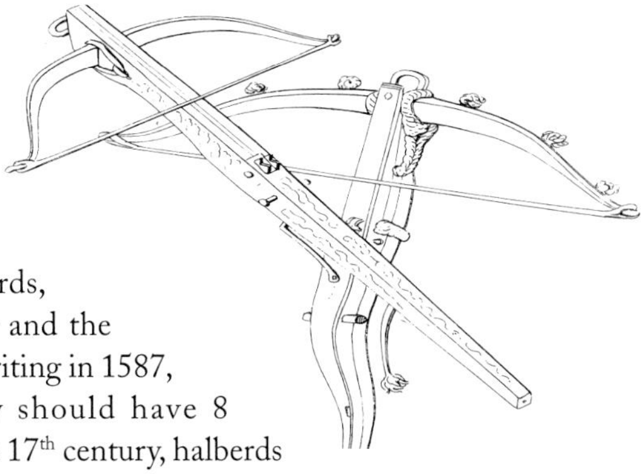

Unlike the bill, halberds remained part of the English armies, though primarily in a ceremonial role. Halberdiers were also assigned as guards, specifically to protect the commander and the ensign, or flag bearer.[92] Barnaby Rich, writing in 1587, believed that a 225-man company should have 8 halberdiers protecting the flag.[93] By the 17th century, halberds and other staff weapons, whose effectiveness diminished with the increasing power of firearms, were processional arms often carried as indicators of rank or, as in the above case, ceremonially.

*Figure 53. Crossbow and bolts.*

## The Bow and Crossbow

The longbow, whose height corresponded to the archer, was embraced by the English in the 13th century and remained the national weapon for both war and hunting to the late 16th century. The English maintained this weapon long after it was abandoned by other countries, its use even encouraged by laws. Proficient use of the English longbow required constant training, and its practice was the only activity allowed on Sundays in Elizabethan England.[94]

The crossbow was more powerful that the longbow. Its missile, known as a bolt, was heavier than the arrow and could deliver a more forceful blow. In addition, the crossbow had greater range and the archer could fire from cramped spaces, not needing to stand up to bend the bow as with the longbow.

*Figure 54. Archer bending the longbow.*

The crossbow was used militarily by the English into the 16th century, but was considered to be not as effective in battle as the longbow. The biggest disadvantage of the weapon was that loading required a spanning mechanism to stretch the string of the bow, thereby requiring a number of time-consuming steps before the bolt could be fired. This handicap was noted in 1539 during Spanish exploration of the New World, when crossbowmen were recorded as able to fire one bolt for every three or four arrows of the Indians.[95]

Long after it was replaced on the battlefield by firearms, the crossbow remained the weapon of the upper classes for hunting deer and rabbits on their private game preserves. For this purpose it was ideal—it was not only

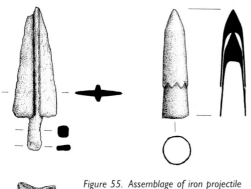

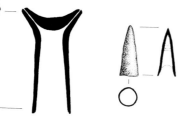

Figure 55. Assemblage of iron projectile points from the fort site. The points at upper left and lower right are for use with a longbow, while the remaining two are crossbow quarrels.

noiseless and powerful, but the bolts comprised reusable ammunition.

It has been the long-held opinion that the colonists did not bring longbows or crossbows with them to Virginia for fear that they might fall into the hands of the Indians. The latter's proven proficiency with stringed projectile weapons, so the thinking went, could be deadly to the colonists if they also acquired the English technology, including steel arrowheads. This belief stems from a 1622 entry in the Virginia Company records. After the massacre which left many colonists dead and the survivors short of the means to defend themselves, the crown offered "the Company for the Virginia Plantacon" some rather obsolete weaponry that was stored in the armory of the Tower of London. Among the objects proposed to be sent were "400 bowes, and bowestaves," and "800 shefs [sheaves] of Arrowes."[96] These are the only items in the gift that the Colony had reservations about accepting and requested that they be diverted to Bermuda for safekeeping.

> The Bowes and Arrowes wch his Matie [Majesty] had giuen to the Virginia Companie (in respect the vse and scatteringe of them amongst the Indians might proue a thinge dangerous in our owne people, and withall make them acquainted with the manner of fashoning the Arrowe heads)that therefore they should be deposited and kept safe in the Sumer Ilands in a readines against there should be occasion to vse them in Virginia.[97]

Recent excavations have shown that while the colonists may have been reluctant to have bows and arrows in 1622, they felt otherwise during the early years of the settlement. Two steel arrowheads and two steel points, or quarrels, to crossbow bolts have been recovered in the fort area.

One of the arrowheads is a short socketed point whose form has been associated with archery practice, since it was easily retrievable from targets, and based on the English sites on which it has been found. This type of point had a long range of manufacture, having been found on English sites dating from the 12th to the 16th century.[98] There is no mention in the documentary records of the Jamestown colonists practicing their archery, but since constant practice was required to be proficient at the bow, it is likely they did.

The second arrowhead is triangular and has a pronounced central re-inforcing spine. It is tanged rather than socketed and, just where the tang is broken off, it appears to be twisted. Forms such as these, that would have been screwed into the wooden shaft of the arrow rather than fitting over it, are found on English sites dating between the 9th and 11th centuries![99] It is doubtful that the Jamestown arrowhead dates this early, and its existence in a post-medieval context poses an anomaly to the established typology of English arrowheads.

The two crossbow bolt quarrels are also not typical of the examples currently in the English record. An X-ray of the first one shows it is pyramidal and socketed, and it appears to be a point within a point. Perhaps the quarrels were stored or shipped stacked one upon another, but the evidence of copper on the upper part suggests that the two points may have been brazed together. In addition, the upper, and outer, quarrel has a scalloped edge not seen on the inner quarrel and may represent an additional method used to attach the two quarrels together. This object, then, appears to be a reinforced crossbow quarrel, but reinforced for what purpose? Certainly it would not be required in hunting where the largest animal to be encountered would be a deer. It seems rather to be designed for warfare and perhaps to be of the strength to have an impact on body armor.

The second crossbow bolt quarrel appears to be of the type used for hunting, but, again, no parallel examples exist in the English material culture record. It is a large robust socketed point with a coronal head of five points. There is a single attachment hole on the shaft for securing the quarrel to the wooden bolt. Bolts with large, heavy heads, such as this, would not have a great range. They were used for hunting small animals such as rabbits—the point designed to batter and stun the animal, not to penetrate the skin and damage the fur. Its association with hunting is also suggested by its similarity to the *Krönenbolzen*, or crowned quarrel, that was used in a competition especially popular on the Continent whereby the target resembles a bird, also known as a popinjay.[100] "Shooting with a crossbow at the popinjay is, perhaps, one of the oldest sports in existence in which the bow is concerned."[101]

## The Halberd

The halberd is an staff weapon of the foot soldier that combined the advantages of the spear and the ax; its name is derived from the combination of two German words: *Halm*, meaning staff, and *Barte*, meaning ax.[102] The halberd was used as early as the 13th century in Switzerland and, as a cutting and thrusting weapon, was particularly effective against cavalry forces.

Unlike the bill, which required no specialized training for its effective use, the halberd, with its slender spike, had to be handled deftly. Early on it seems to have been reserved for officers with special training. Again

Figure 56. Engraving showing halberdiers guarding a ceremonial procession.

Humphrey Barwick states:

> I wish no Halbardes into the handes of any that hath no skill to use the same, for it is a weapon that can abide no blowes, as the Bill will doo, but yet in the handes of officers, and such as hath skill how to use the same, it is a very good weapon, but the same must be handled delicately with the push only and quicklie drawed backe.[103]

Over the years, the design of the halberd was modified to increase its effectiveness and, because it became a weapon of the gentlemen officers, to incorporate surface decoration. By the mid-16th century the halberd's wide ax-like blade with forward sloping edge developed into a lighter crescent-shaped blade, often decoratively pierced and etched.

Halberds were carried by sergeants as a sign of rank and to signal commands to their companies. The 1612 martial laws for the Jamestown colony required the sergeants to carry halberds for garrison duty but to abandon them for firearms in the field, "onely the Serieant in Garrison shall vse his Halbert, and in field his Snaphaunse and Target."[104] By this time, the "halberd" had become synonymous with "Sergeant," as seen in the same martial laws which state that the "Captaine who shall dispose of a Halbert, by vertue whereof a Serjeant is known…."[105]

Halberdiers were employed at Jamestown in 1610 as special guards to Governor De La Warr, who embraced the pomp and ceremony of his office in his efforts to rediscipline and revitalize the flagging colony. Every Sunday, on De La Warr's march to church, he was:

> accompanied with all the councilors, captains, other officers, and all the gentlemen, and with a guard of halberdiers in His Lordship's livery, fair red cloaks, to the number of fifty, both on each side and behind him.[106]

One halberd blade has been excavated during excavations of the fort site, which may be a remnant of one of De La Warr's halberdiers. It was located in Pit 4, which was only briefly tested before the completion of the excavation season, but it appears to date similarly to Pits 1 and 3 (c.1610). The blade is crescent shaped, and it is decorated with conic and biconic piercing creating four dolphins. The surface appears to have been decoratively engraved and incorporates projections on the top and bottom of the blade which are the heads of griffin-like beasts. Halberds are not common finds on Virginia archaeological sites. Only one other was unearthed at Jamestown during the National Park Service excavations.

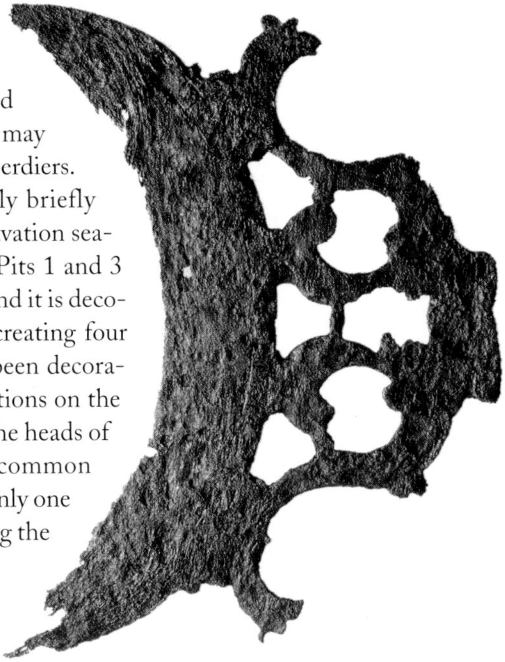

*Figure 57. Decorative halberd blade excavated from Pit 4.*

## Accoutrements

In the 1590s, Humphrey Barwick was an old soldier who had served in England, France, Scotland, and Spain. Barwick authored a book on military affairs, advocating the use of firearms instead of the longbow, in which he described the items that a well-equipped "shot" of the infantry should carry "to keepe [his weapon] cleane and cleere as well within as without." These include "his scrues and wormes to serve all for his skowring sticke…and a priming Iron for the clearinge of the tuch hole."[107]

Each of these objects—the scourer, the worm, and the priming wire—has been recovered from the *Jamestown Rediscovery* excavations. The scourer and worm represent especially rare finds, for while they "formed part of a standard musketman's kit [they] do not normally survive even in armouries."[108] Both of these tools would be attached to the end of the wooden scouring stick, the other end of which would serve as a ramrod to push the lead ball into the breech (closed end) of the firearm barrel. The scourer was specifically used to clean the powder scale from the inside of the barrel. This would build up with use, especially when using poor quality gunpowder, and interfere with proper ignition of the charge. The head of the scourer, which was found in Pit 1, is divided into three blades: a central straight one, which would be "trimmed on the end with a linen cloth of sufficient substance"[109] to wipe the interior

*Figure 58. Firearm scourer from Pit 1.*

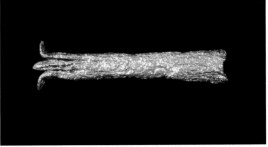

*Figure 59. Firearm worm from Pit 3.*

of the barrel, flanked by two angled blades for scraping the same. The scourer would have fit a barrel with an interior diameter of 22 mm and is socketed for the insertion of the scouring rod. There is a rectangular attachment slot on the side, which suggests that the rod was not meant to be removable and was permanently attached. This is different from the later known examples, such as the scourer illustrated in Wallhausen's *Kriegskunst zu Fuss* (1615) and the one excavated from nearby Martin's Hundred (c.1620-22), which have a screw attachment on one end.

A worm was excavated from Pit 3, like Pit 1, a context dating to 1610. This worm has screw threads on one end and a corkscrew head with a double twist. It would have been used to pull out wet powder as well as the paper wadding used to keep the ball and powder in the barrel.

Fragments of two brass prickers, or priming wires, for cleaning out the firearm's touchhole were also found in Pit 1. The touchhole or vent is the small hole through the barrel at the breech leading from the pan. It is through this hole that the lighted gunpowder in the pan ignites the powder in the barrel. If this touchhole becomes clogged with burned powder, the weapon will misfire. The two prickers from the pit each consist of thin brass wire, 2 mm in diameter, which is twisted on one end. It is not known how long the two objects were, as the "pricker end," which was probably twisted to form a point, has broken off. A similar priming wire was excavated from the 1629 shipwreck *Batavia*.[110]

Barwick also stated in his description of well-armed soldiers that the harquebusier must have "a purse for his bullets."[111] A separate bag, worn on the bandolier or suspended from a waist belt, would have held the lead balls prior to loading the firearm. The frame from one of these bullet bags was recovered from Pit 1. It contains iron rivets for the attachment of the leather bag and has an iron buckle on a spring permitting quick release of the bag from its belt. A parallel has not been found for this type of quick-

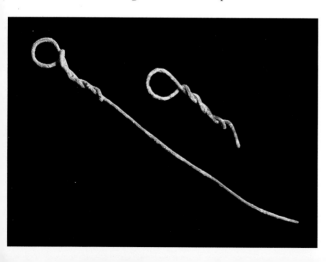

*Figure 60. Two brass prickers from Pit 1 for cleaning the firearm touchhole.*

*Figure 61. Iron frame with a quick-release buckle (below) from a bullet bag similar to the one seen on the waist belt of Charles V of Spain in a mid-16th-century painting (above and detail, left).*

release bullet bag among English collections, but a 1546 painting by Titian appears to depict Charles V of Spain wearing a similar one on a waist belt.

Other accoutrements required for firearms, such as bandoliers, bullet molds, and bullets, have been found during *Jamestown Rediscovery* excavations. A 1601 English arms delivery for the army in Ireland included matchlock muskets and calivers furnished with both matchlock and snaphaunce locks.[112] All the snaphaunce calivers were to be equipped with two powder flasks, one containing powder for the barrel and a smaller one containing the priming powder. All the matchlocks, however, were to be supplied with "bandaleeres of double plate." Developed in the Netherlands

*Figure 62. Lead bandolier cap (above) and a sample of the brass and iron bandolier cylinders (right) from the fort site.*

by 1550, the bandolier consisted of a leather strap worn across one shoulder from which usually hung 12 cylinders, each containing enough gunpowder for one shot (see figure 47). Most commonly made of wood, they also were made of iron and brass. Sometimes the wood cylinders were covered in leather, but it is assumed that the iron cylinders were always covered with leather or some other material to prevent making a spark and igniting the powder they were carrying. Brass would not pose this problem but covered brass cylinders are found in museum collections and may indicate an attempt to muffle the rattling. Leather does not survive in most archaeological contexts and was not found covering the Jamestown cylinders, but many leather-covered iron bandolier cylinders are part of the Nova Zembla collection of 1595. There is also an elaborate bandolier in the Royal Armouries, made about 1605, that has tinned iron cylinders covered with velvet.[113]

The *Jamestown Rediscovery* excavations have recovered over 30 bandolier cylinders, only four of which are brass. The iron cylinders all show signs of tinning, which reflects the reference to "double plate" on the bandoliers bound for Ireland, and must have been applied to help prevent the material from corroding.

Bandolier cylinders have caps with ear-like projections through which strings from the bandolier belt were fitted. These allowed the caps to easily slide up and down, opening and closing the cylinders, without fear of losing the caps. Some of the Jamestown bandolier cylinders have been found bearing their caps, which are always of the same material as the cylinders. Although no documentary reference has been found for the use of lead for these caps, large numbers of cast lead bandolier caps have been found on English, Virginia, and Maryland sites from c. 1620 to 1650. Three of these lead caps have been found by *Jamestown Rediscovery*, also from second quarter 17th-century features. On all the sites where these have been located there have never been any matching cylinders of lead which, from the weight alone, would be a very unsatisfactory material for a bandolier. From the records we know that the caps presented a problem in that they were easily opened by body movement or entanglement in underbrush. This would expose the powder, thereby subjecting the soldier to the possibility of priming flash. The wooden cylinder caps, especially, must have presented a problem in changing climates that would cause them to shrink and swell, keeping them from fitting securely. Perhaps the lead caps are an easy and inexpensive way to replace the wooden caps once they have become unserviceable.

Even though the bandolier was convenient for loading the matchlock, it also had a number of disadvantages, which eventually led to its abandonment. The main problems included the design of the bandolier, which encircles the soldier's body with highly combustible power making him susceptible to burns; the tendency of soldiers to get ensnared in the suspension strings while trying to quickly reload; and the noise the cylinders made knocking together. These issues are summed up by military writer Roger, Earl of Orrery:

> Besides, I have often seen much prejudice in the use of bandeleers,
> which being worn in the belts for them, above the soldiers' coats are
> often apt to take fire, especially if the matchlock musket be used; and
> when they take fire, they commonly wound and often kill him that
> wears them, and those near him: for likely if one bandeleer take
> fire, all the rest do in that collar: they often tangle those which use
> them on service, when they have fired, and on falling off by the
> flanks of the files of the intervals, to get into the rear to charge
> again. To which I shall add, that in secret attempts in the night,
> their rattling often discovers the design, and enables the enemy to
> prevent it; and in the day time on service, especially if the weather
> be windy, their rattling also too frequently hinders the soldiers from
> hearing, and consequently obeying the officer's word of command,
> which must be fatal when it happens.[114]

His analysis of Orrery was made in 1677, so despite all its disadvantages, the bandolier continued to be used into the late 17th century. Leather-covered metal bandolier cylinders recently have been excavated from a 1690 shipwreck, *Anse aux Bouleaux*, of the siege of Quebec.[115]

Evidence of ten musket rests, used to steady the aim of the 16-20 pound matchlock musket, have been excavated so far. Consisting of the top sec-

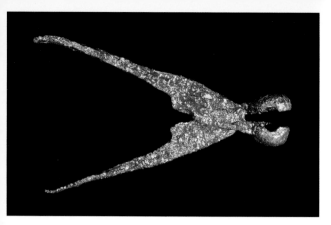

*Figure 63. Iron bullet mold for casting a single lead ball.*

tion only, they are each of similar construction, exhibiting a U-shaped fork with curling terminals. A separate ferrule is secured to the fork's scale tang by an screw eye, which also would have penetrated the wooden pole upon which the fork was seated. From the eye there would have been tied "double stringes…to hang about the arme of the souldier when at anytime he shall have occasion to traile the same."[116] Some of the 1607 de Gheyn drawings of the musketeer depict the soldier dragging his musket rest by this cord as he loads his weapon with powder. The musket rest began going out of use in the 1640s, when the lighter musket was adopted and the rest was no longer required.

Also part of the arms accoutrements are nine scissors-type bullet molds. They all have integral sprue cutters which would have been used to cut off the excess casting lead. This is an important step since an unbalanced ball could have an irregular trajectory,[117] and a ball still bearing sprue may not load into the weapon properly. Barwick advises the harqubusier to mold his bullets "as round as is possible, and the same well pared, to that ende it may fall close to the powder, without staying by the way."[118]

The molds would have cast balls of 15 and 17 mm in diameter. Only one ball of this size would be loaded into the barrel of the firearm, but the charge could also include a handful of smaller shot ranging in size from 1 to 10 mm in diameter. The small shot was produced in two ways at Jamestown. One method was in a gang mold which, as the name suggests, can cast a number of shot at one time and usually in varying sizes. It is obvious that the colonists had these molds, as evidenced by the large number of the small lead shot with mold seams and by the many shot still attached to runners of lead created in the molding process. Gang molds from this time period rarely are found archaeologically. This may be explained by the fact that they were often made of breakable slate or soapstone.[119]

The other method of producing shot was by pouring molten lead through a copper

*Figure 64. Lead shot still attached to the runner of casting lead created in a gang mold.*

strainer into a pail of water. This was a process widely used from the mid-16th century through the 18th century. Writing of this procedure in the late 17th century, German Prince Rupert cautions that as "long as you observe the right temper of the heat, the Lead will constantly drop into very round shot, without so much as one with a tail in many pounds." If the shot "fall to be round and without tail, there is Auripigmentum (arsenic trisulphide) enough put in and the temper of the heat is right."[120] Many pieces of small shot from the excavations exhibit these tails, indicating that the colonists had difficulties in either regulating the heat or in the correct proportion of ingredients.

The strainer used to melt the shot is described by Rupert as a "round plate of Copper…the hollow whereof is to be about three inches over, the bottom lower then the brims about half an inch, pierced with thirty, forty or more small holes."[121] References to these objects can be seen in the records. Humphrey Barwick in 1594 wants "every tenn souldiers to have a casting panne."[122] The Virginia Company Records of 1618 specify that for every 35 men sent to Virginia there should be "Six hun. Wt of lead and melting pans 3."[123] During excavations of Pit 3, hardened lead residue from the interior of one of these melting or casting pans was located. It is rectangular with a number of tiny holes punched in the bottom, most of them still clogged with shot. The residue has taken shape around a tool that was being used in an attempt to force cooling lead through the strainer.

Figure 65. Small lead shot exhibiting the "tails" created by dripping the molten lead through a strainer into a container of water.

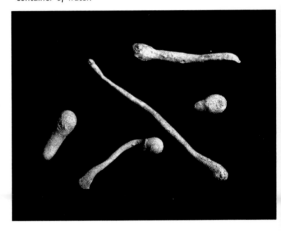

Figure 66. Both sides of lead residue with impressions of the strainer through which the cooling lead was being forced in an attempt to make shot.

# Jamestown Portrait

The English soldiers that arrived at Jamestown likely had varied backgrounds. Some likely saw action in 1600 at the Battle of Nieuport, a major infantry engagement in the Netherlands when more than 13,000 English and Dutch soldiers inflicted a crushing defeat on the Spanish forces. Others quite possibly were veterans of the highly unpopular wars against the Irish forces of the Earl of Tyrone. Some may have had militia training, and others were gentlemen volunteers, the younger sons of the gentry.

The first contingent that landed in 1607 were under the command of Edward Wingfield, President of the Council and also a veteran of both Ireland and the Low Countries. Initially, Wingfield set his men about constructing a flimsy fortification, but, curiously, did not permit "exercise at armes" during the first weeks.[124] These decisions may have been influenced by Wingfield's experience in Ireland, believing that only light fortifications were necessary against the Powhatan, an adversary that fought much like the Irish. And if the English were not going to fight in massed formations, perhaps musket drills might not seem so imperative. However, it is difficult to understand why Wingfield did not even order the weapons to be removed from their shipping casks. Only after a devastating Indian attack two weeks later, that killed one boy and wounded 17 colonists, did Wingfield allow "…his men armed and exercised." This neglect apparently continued until September 1608 when the newly elected President John Smith had "…the order of the watch renewed, the squadrons (each setting of the watch) trained; the whole Company every Saturday exercised, in the plaine by the west Bulwarke, prepared for that purpose, we called Smithfield…." The colonists took this opportunity to make an intentional show of their firepower at one of the Saturday exercises to impress visiting Indians when "…a fyle would batter a tree," though "file" seems to be confused with "rank" in this passage.[125]

Shooting by rank and file was a complicated and potentially dangerous maneuver that required regular practice. In fact, just loading and firing a musket was an elaborate process. By 1611, however, powder was so precious that musket training was limited to "false firing," in which the musket was not loaded, but only the pan was primed and discharged.[126] In addition to firearms training, the Saturday exercises may also have included pike drills. The English were constantly concerned about a Spanish attack on Jamestown, and the pikeheads found by the *Jamestown Rediscovery* excavations suggest that the colonists were prepared to defend themselves against enemies using European methods of warfare. However, at least one man held the English soldiers at Jamestown in low regard. Don Diego de Molina's stated that, "Nor are they efficient soldiers, although the rulers and captains make a great profession of this because of the time they served in Flanders on the side of Holland, where some have companies and castles. The men are poorly drilled and not prepared for military action." This opinion may not be entirely objective since Molina was a Spanish agent imprisoned in Virginia for five years.[127] Interestingly, there is archaeological evidence that Jamestown soldiers were well disciplined, at least when it came to one aspect of sentry duty. The excavations have produced numerous large lead bullets that are covered with tooth marks, undoubtedly the result of the fact that sentries were required to have their weapons charged and to keep bullets in their mouths.[128]

Figure 67. One of many lead balls recovered from the site exhibiting tooth impressions, probably the result of bored sentries following prescribed military procedures requiring them to keep bullets ready for firing by holding them in their mouths.

There is a good picture of the military disposition of Jamestown in 1610 after the arrival of Lord De La Warr, the new governor.[129] Sir Thomas Gates became Lieutenant General in charge of all officers and soldiers, including their training. George Percy became captain of the fort's 50 man garrison. Sir Fernando Wainman became Master of the Ordnance. As the title suggests, Wainman was responsible for all the artillery, powder, and shot, including munitions, for all soldiers carrying firearms. In addition, the Master of the Ordnance was usually in charge of constructing and maintaining fortifications. Captain George Webb became Sergeant Major of the fort. Sergeant Majors typically were soldiers with extensive experience, since their main duty was to direct the disposition of forces in battle. As Sergeant Major, Captain Webb was responsible for the security of James Fort, making assignments for the "Court of Guard" and establishing the watchword. Edward Brewster was in charge of the governor's guard of halberdiers, who served as the governor's personal bodyguard and carried his banners. The ornate halberd uncovered at Jamestown surely indicates that the military custom of using halberds as ceremonial weapons, carried by sergeants and the color guard, was brought to Jamestown.

Of course, there were captains to command the troops. George Yeardley became captain of Thomas Gates' company, and Samuel Argall, Thomas Holecroft, and Thomas Lawson each became captain of a 50-man militia company. If they were like Old World officers, Captains Yeardley, Argall, Holecroft, and Lawson were expected to lead their men in battle, but probably not to decide on the tactics, which were the Sergeant Major's forte. Unnamed were the sergeants, corporals, and ensigns, as well as the common soldiers. Their duties included guarding the island and the fort, protecting workers in the field, serving on exploratory and trading expeditions, garrisoning outposts such as Algernon Fort and Fort Charles at Point Comfort and the block house on Hog Island, serving on expeditions against the Virginia Indians, and, it seems, laboring as husbandmen.

*Figure 68. Soldiers equipped with longbow, sword and target, and halberd. All this weaponry was used at Jamestown, although it was considered obsolete for military forces in England by the 17th century.*

The Virginia experience was unique for the English soldier, though it had some similarities to military ventures in Ireland and expeditions to Roanoke Island. So it is not surprising that adaptations were made to traditional military practices, at least by skillful leaders. Perhaps the most conspicuous example of English adjustment was abandoning the use of massed soldiers in rank and file for more "unconventional" warfare when fighting the Virginia Indians. The ever resourceful John Smith, whose combat experience was in Europe and not Ireland, instructed his men in guerrilla warfare:

> *"Sixe or seaven daies we spent only in tranying our men to march, fight, and scirmish in the woods. These willing minds to this action, so quickned their understanding in this exercise, as in all judgements wee were better able to fight with Powhatan's whole force in our order of battle amongst the Trees (for Thicks there are few) then the Fort was to repulse 400 at the first assault, with some tenne or twenty shot, not knowing what to doe, or how to use a Piece."*[30]

Since Smith's men were skirmishing and not firing from ranks, the soldiers had to get closer to their targets to have a better chance of hitting one. This meant an increased need for mobility; that, in turn, suggests the men likely were equipped with calivers rather than heavy muskets and were not wearing plate armor, but either brigandines or jack coats. The use of light body protection was evidenced in Smith's voyage to meet Powhatan at Werowicomico when Smith went ashore with "…20 shot armed in Jacks."[131]

Another major lesson that the English learned was an apparent renewed appreciation for a long since obsolete piece of equipment known as a target. Targets were a type of shield that were carried by pikemen, although by the mid-1500s they were no longer favored by troops for "…neither is there almost any man that will burden himself with it except captains." However, targeteers are employed in small numbers in Ireland as late as 1600, apparently as scouts and to cover soldiers with firearms in skirmishes,[132] as well as leading assaults on lightly fortified positions when mobility is presumably at a premium.[133] Robert Barret suggested that soldiers armed with targets, a short sword, and pistol were the best way to creep along trenches and enter into mines.[134] While targets were not a very practical defense against Spanish muskets, they were valuable in hand-to-hand fighting and they clearly could stop Virginia Indian arrows. This was graphically demonstrated during an expedition up the Nansemond

River when Smith and his comrades were attacked from both sides of the river with "…arrowes so fast as two or three hundred could shoot them." None of the English were seriously wounded, probably because "More than one hundred arrowes stucke in our Targets, and about the boat."[135] Smith carried a target as part of his personal equipment, as did Rawley Crashaw.[136] If the instructions in the 1611 Martial Laws were faithfully carried out, officers carried targets, and certain soldiers were outfitted as "Targiteers."[137]

Although perhaps only 12% of James Fort has been excavated by *Jamestown Rediscovery*, the excavations are making substantial new contributions to understanding the past. Many of the objects being recovered are not necessarily represented in English collections. This is because in the first fifteen years of its existence, while under Virginia Company control, Jamestown was a bit of a "dumping ground" for England's excesses, including obsolete arms and armor. Mention has already been made of the Royal Armory cleaning out its store of arms for the hapless colonists after the 1622 massacre. This weaponry was donated because it is described by the Master of the Ordnance as "being vnfitt for any moderne service here."[138] This pattern of distribution has resulted in many rare and unusual objects clustering in the Jamestown colony.

*Figure 69.*

# Endnotes

[1] Douglas Owsley, *Bioarchaeological Research at Jamestown*, in William M. Kelso and Beverly Straube, *1996 Interim Report on the APVA Excavations at Jamestown, Virginia* (Richmond, VA: Association for the Preservation of Virginia Antiquities, 1997), 27-29.

[2] Philip L. Barbour, ed., *The Complete Works of Captain John Smith (1580-1631)* (Chapel Hill: The Univ. of North Carolina Press, 1986), II:140-141.

[3] Owsley, 28.

[4] At this writing the skeleton is still embedded in the clay, so that it is possible that when the bones are removed, other injuries may be detected on the opposite side of the bones.

[5] Ballistic tests at close range seem to rule out any self-inflicted accidental wounding at close range. See page 14.

[6] George Percy, [1608?] *Observations gathered out of "A Discourse of the Southern Colony in Virginia by the English, 1606,"* ed. David B. Quinn (Charlottesville, VA: Univ. Press of Virginia, 1967), 24.

[7] Ibid.

[8] Ibid., 25.

[9] Barbour, II:139.

[10] Dr. S.E. Sutton, *The First Virginia Colonists*, report of June 10, 1988, for the Jamestown-Yorktown Foundation, Williamsburg Virginia, np. The author is indebted to Mrs. Nancy Egloff, research historian for the Jamestown Settlement, for sharing this information.

[11] Douglas Owsley, personal communication.

[12] Ibid.

[13] Barbour, II:139.

[14] Jocelyn R. Wingfield, *Virginia's True Founder* (Athens, Georgia: The Wingfield Family Society, 1993), 176-177.

[15] Virginia M. Meyer and John Frederick Dorman, *Adventurers of Purse and Person*, 3rd ed. (Richmond, VA: Order of First Families of Virginia, 1987), 586.

[16] Edward Duffield Neill, *Virginia Carolum* (Albany, NY: 1886), 88.

[17] Barbour, I:20.

[18] Samuel H. Yonge, *The Site of Old Jamestown* (Richmond, VA: APVA, 1903), 72.

[19] We are indebted to Dr. David Hunt, forensic anthropologist, Smithsonian Institution for mending the skull.

[20] Lucy Tomlin Smith, *The Itinerary of John Leland, 1535-1543* (Carbondale, Il: Southern Illinois Univ. Press, 1964), 47, 49, 59.

[21] William M. Kelso, *Jamestown Rediscovery I* (Richmond, VA: APVA, 1995) and William M. Kelso, *Jamestown Rediscovery II* (Richmond, VA: APVA, 1996), passim.

[22] Barbour, II:175.

[23] Gabriel Archer, *A Relayton of the Discovery*, in Edward Arber, ed., *John Smith's Works* (Birmingham: King's College, 1884), I:lii-lv.

[24] I am indebted to Dennis Blanton, Center for Archaeological Research, College of William and Mary, for assessing the collection.

[25] Archer, lii.

[26] Australian Surveying & Land Information Group, Department of Industry, Science and Tourism, Belconnen, ACT, Australia, Blanton.

[27] Percy, 26.

[28] For a discussion of how similar the English and Native Americans were in pre-industrial revolution Virginia and yet how cultural-centric they both were, see Nancy Oestreich Lurie, *Indian Cultural Adjustment to European Civilization*, in James Morton Smith, ed., *Seventeen Century America* (Chapel Hill: Univ. of North Corolina Press, 1959), 33-60.

[29] Owsley, personal communication. This is his preliminary field analysis.

[30] Emily Williams, Archaeological Conservator, Colonial Williamsburg Foundation, letter to Elliott Jordan, March 5, 1998.

[31] Barbour, II:192.

[32] Meyer and Dorman, 51.

[33] We are indebted to Dr. Harry Hager and Bruce Wilson for providing the Computed Tomography (CT) scan at Williamsburg Community Hospital; Marc McAllister of Innova, International, Dallas, Texas, for processing the CT data into a stereolithography file; and Accelerated Technologies for building the model.

[34] John L. Cotter, *Archeological Excavations at Jamestown, Virginia*, reprint of 1958 edition (Washington, D.C.: U.S. Department of the Interior, 1994), 219-225.

[35] Ibid., 22-24. Douglas Owsley, Parvene Hamzavi, and Karin L. Bruwelheide, *Analysis of the APVA Skeletal Collection, Jamestown, VA* (National Park Service, mss, 1997), 1-12.

[36] Another estimate suggests that about 210 died that winter out of a total population of 270. Nancy Egloff, *Memorandum to the Interpretive Staff at Jamestown Settlement*, April 10, 1990.

[37] David W. Stahle, et al, "The Lost Colony and Jamestown Droughts," *Science*, April 24, 1998.

[38] For details on this construction see David F. Riggs, *Embattled Shrine* (Shippensburg, PA: White Maine Publishing Co.,1997).

[39] Barbour, I:233, 325.

[40] Because Ralph Hamor used the word "reduced" to describe an obviously enlarged town, that must have been the case.

[41] Barbour, II:324.

[42] William Strachey, "A True Reportory of the Wreck and Redemption of Sir Thomas Gates, Knight," in *A Voyage to Virginia in 1609*, ed. Louis B. Wright (Charlottesville, VA: Univ. Press of Virginia, 1964), 63-64.

[43] Ralph Hamor, "A True Discourse of the Present Estate of Virginia, and the successe of the Affaires there till the 18 of June, 1615," in Barbour, II:242.

[44] This object, known as a spatula mundani, is discussed in detail by curator Beverly Straube in William M. Kelso, Nicholas M. Luccketti, and Beverly A. Straube, *Jamestown Rediscovery III* (Richmond, VA: APVA, 1997), 46-47.

[45] Strachey, "True Reportory," 79-80.

[46] Kelso, Luccketti, Straube, *Jamestown Rediscovery III*, 8-9.

[47] Warren Billings, *Jamestown and the Founding of the Nation* (Gettysburg, PA: Thomas Publications, nd), 73, and William Waller Hening, *The Statutes at Large*, (Charlottesville, VA: Univ. of Virginia Press, 1969), I:206.

[48] I am indebted to Mr. John Allan of Exeter Museum for leading me to this interesting building.

[49] Testing done by Beta Analytical Inc., February 19, 1998, Sample 1: 2000 +/- 40 BP, Sample 2: 2140 +/-40 BP.

[50] Professor Jerre Johnson, Chairman, Department of Geology, College of William and Mary, was kind enough to conduct these tests. He feels that the preliminary tests could also be interpreted to show that an eroding ravine would make it more difficult to determine the 1607 shoreline. Future, more complete tests are planned.

[51] Barbour, I:273.

[52] Ibid., II:140-142.

[53] Ibid.,I: 222-223, 241-242.

[54] Percy, 24-25

[55] Barbour, I:224.

[56] Ibid., I:230.

[57] Ibid., I:230.

[58] Correlli Barnet, *Britain and Her Army* (London: Allen Lane The Penquin Press, 1970), 23.

[59] Ibid., 34.

[60] Ibid., 32-33

[61] C. G. Cruickshank, *Elizabeth's Army* (London: Oxford Univ. Press, 1946), 8-9.

[62] Ibid., 60-61. Also J. J. N. McGurk, "Life in the Elizabethan Army," *British History Illustrated* 2 no. 6 (Feb 1976): 16-25.

[63] Henry J. Webb, *Elizabethan Military Science* (Madison, WI: The Univ. of Wisconsin Press, 1965), 78-86. Barnet, 45-47.

[64] Ibid., 68-69.

[65] James Lavin, personal communication, 1997.

[66] Robert Barret, [1598] *The Theorike and Practike of Moderne Warres* (New York: Da Capo Press, 1969), 2.

[67] Ibid., 33.

[68] Barbour, I:270.

[69] Ibid., I:237.

[70] Bert S. Hall, *Weapons and Warfare in Renaissance Europe* (Baltimore, MD: Johns Hopkins Univ. Press, 1997), 139-140.

[71] Humphrey Barwick, [1594] *A breefe discourse, concerning the force of all manuall weapons of fire* (Norwood, NJ: Walter J. Johnson, 1974), 8.

[72] Howard L. Blackmore, *British Military Firearms 1650-1850* (London: Herbert Jenkins,1961),18.

[73] Barbour, II:144.

[74] Barwick, 18.

[75] Geoffrey Boothroyd, "The Birth of the Scottish Pistol, " in *Scottish Weapons and Fortifications 1100-1800*, ed. David H. Caldwell (Edinburgh: John Donald Publishers, Ltd., 1981), 35.

[76] Harold Peterson, *Arms and Armor in Colonial America 1526-1783*, (New York: Bramhall House,1956), 26.

[77] Barbour, I:45.

[78] Ibid., I:51.

[79] John McGurk, *The Elizabethan Conquest of Ireland* (Manchester: Manchester Univ. Press, 1997), 228.

80 J.B. Kist, *Jacob de Gheyn, The Exercise of Arms* (New York: McGraw-Hill, 1971), 30.

81 McGurk, *Conquest of Ireland*, 230.

82 Cyril Falls, *Elizabeth's Irish Wars*, (London: Methuen & Co., 1950), 60-61.

83 David Quinn, *New American World, A Documentary History of North America to 1612* (New York: Arno Press & Hector Bye, Inc., 1979), V:276.

84 Susan M. Kingsbury, ed., *The Records of the Virginia Company of London* (Washington: Government Printing Office, 1906), III:447.

85 David Blackmore, *Arms & Armour of the English Civil Wars* (London: Royal Armouries, 1990), 75.

86 J.B. Kist, personal communication, 1998.

87 Barbour, II:187.

88 David B. Quinn, "Preparations for the 1585 Virginia Voyage," *William and Mary Quarterly*, 3rd Series, VI, no. 2 (April 1949): 212.

89 McGurk, *Conquest of Ireland*, 227.

90 Webb, 91.

91 Cruickshank, 61.

92 Webb, 91-92.

93 Falls, 43.

94 Christopher Hibbert, *Agincort* (New York: Dorset Press, 1964), 35-36.

95 Peterson, 11.

96 Kingsbury, III:676.

97 Kingsbury, II:100.

98 Oliver Jessop, "A New Artefact Typology for the Study of Medieval Arrowheads," *Medieval Archaeology* XL (1996): 197.

99 Jessop, 195.

100 Josef Alm, *European Crossbows: A Survey*, trans. H. Bartlett Wells, ed. G.M. Wilson (London: 1934), 62-63.

101 Ralph Payne-Gallwey, *The Crossbow* (London: The Holland Press, 1995), 225.

102 Leonid Tarassuk and Claude Blair, eds., *The Complete Encyclopedia of Arms & Weapons* (New York: Bonanza, 1986), 246.

103 Barwick, 23.

104 William Stratchey, [1611] "For the Colony in Virginea Britanniea. Lawes Divine, Morall and Martiall, etc.," in Peter Force, ed., *Tracts and other Papers* (Washington: Wm. Q. Force, 1844), 32.

105 Strachey, "Lawes Divine, Morall and Martiall," 50.

106 Strachey, "True Reportory," 80.

107 Barwick, 8.

108 Paul Courtney, "The Medieval and Post-Medieval Objects," in Peter Ellis, ed., *Beeston Castle, Cheshire* (London: English Heritage, 1993), 157.

109 Peterson, 41.

110 Jeremy N. Green, *The loss of the Verenigde Oostindische Compagnie retourschip "Batavia," Western Australia 1629* (BAR International Series 489, 1989), 72.

111 Barwick, 9.

112 Howard Blackmore, 17-18.

113 David Blackmore, 72.

114 Peterson, 63.

115 www.mcc.gouv.qc.ca/phips.

116 Gervase Markham, [1625] "Souldiers Accidence" in David Blackmore, 18.

117 M.L. Brown, *Firearms in Colonial America* (Washington: Smithsonian Institution, 1980), 13.

118 Barwick, 8.

119 Peterson, 243.

120 Brown, 64-65.

121 Ibid., 64.

122 Ibid., 8.

123 Kingsbury, II:96.

124 Barbour, II:181.

125 Ibid., II:181.

126 Strachey, "Lawes Divine, Morall and Martiall," 31.

127 Lyon Gardiner Tyler, ed., *Narratives of Early Virginia, 1606-1625*, (New York: Barnes & Noble, 1946), 221.

128 Strachey, "Lawes Divine, Morall and Martiall," 60.

129 Strachey, "True Reportory," 85.

130 Barbour, I:85.

131 Ibid., I:63.

132 Webb, 89-90.

133 McGurk, *Conquest of Ireland*, 228.

134 Barret, 5.

135 Barbour, II:179.

136 Ibid., I: 71.

137 Strachey, "Lawes Divine, Morall and Martiall," 32.

138 Kingsbury, III: 676.

# Illustration Credits

Title Page: Copyright David M. Doody

Figure 1: *The Sentry* by Carel Fabritius, 1654, oil on canvas, 68 x 58 cm, courtesy of Staatliches Museum Shwerin, Shwerin.

Figure 6: *Portrait of George Percy* #854.2, courtesy of Virginia Historical Society, Richmond, VA.

Figure 7: Baptismal Record of St Peter Mancroft, 1585. Courtesy of Norfolk Record Office, Norwich.

Figure 8: *Summer Harvest* c. 1615-20 by Bruegel the younger, Flemish, oil on wood panel, 17¼" x 23¼" (43.8 x 59.0cm). The Nelson-Atkins Museum of Art, Kansas City, Missouri (Purchase: Nelson Trust).

Figure 10: Plate from *The Exerciseof Arms* by Jacob de Gheyn from F. W. H. Hollstein, *Dutch and Flemish Etchings Engravings and Woodcuts ca. 1450-1700* (Amsterdam: Menno Hertzberger, 1949), VII:139.

Figure 20: *Indian Elder or Chief* by John White, c. 1585. Copyright British Museum.

Figure 23: *Indian Village of Pomeiooc* by John White, c. 1585. Copyright British Museum.

Figure 25: *Oderatus* by Frederik Bloemaert, born 1610, from F. W. H. Hollstein, *Dutch and Flemish Etchings Engravings and Woodcuts ca. 1450-1700* (Amsterdam: Menno Hertzberger, 1949), II:90.

Figure 27: *Pocahontas* by Mary Ellen Howe, 1994. Oil on tapestry paper, from an engraving by Simon de Passe. On loan to the Virginia Historical Society, Richmond, VA.

Figure 29: Courtesy National Park Service, Colonial National Historical Park.

Figure 31: adapted from graphic by Dave Herring, Christian Science Monitor, December 23, 1996.

Figure 37: Courtesy National Park Service, Colonial National Historical Park.

Figure 43: Algemeen Rijksarchief, Den Haag, Netherlands.

Figure 46: Reproduced by permission of Edinburgh University Library from John Derrick's *The Image of Ireland*, 1581(De.3.76).

Figure 47: Plate from *The Exerciseof Arms* by Jacob de Gheyn, private collection.

Figure 52: Reproduced by permission of Edinburgh University Library from John Derrick's *The Image of Ireland*, 1581 (De.3.76).

Figure 61: *The Emperor Charles V(1500-58) at the Battle of Muhlberg, 24 April 1547* by Tiziano Vecellio (Titian) Scala, Florence. Copyright Museo del Prado-Madrid-all rights reserved. Reproduction in part or total is prohibited.

Figure 69: *Marching Soldiers, in the Centre a Standard-Bearer* by Jan Theodor de Bry from F. W. H. Hollstein, *Dutch and Flemish Etchings Engravings and Woodcuts ca. 1450-1700* (Amsterdam: Menno Hertzberger, 1949), IV:35.

# Selected Reading

Barbour, Philip L., editor. *The Complete Works of Captain John Smith (1580-1631)*. 3 Volumes. Chapel Hill: University of North Carolina Press, 1986.

Billings, Warren. *Jamestown and the Founding of the Nation*. Gettysburg: Colonial National Historical Park and Eastern National, 1991.

Cotter, John L. *Archaeological Excavations at Jamestown, Virginia*. Washington, D.C.: National Park Service, 1958.

Deetz, James. *Flowerdew Hundred*. Charlottesville, VA: University Press of Virginia, 1993.

Hantman, Jeffrey L. "Between Powhatan and Quirank: Reconstructing Monacan Culture and History in the Context of Jamestown." *American Anthropologist* 92 (1990):676-690.

Harrington, Jean Carl. *An Outwork at Fort Raleigh*. Gettysburg: Eastern National Parks and Monument Association, 1966.

Kelso, William M. *Kingsmill Plantations, 1619-1800*. San Francisco: Academic Press, 1984.

    *Jamestown Rediscovery I*. Richmond, VA: APVA, 1995.

    *Jamestown Rediscovery II*. Richmond, VA: APVA, 1996.

    *Jamestown Rediscovery III*. Richmond, VA: APVA, 1997.

Kupperman, Karen Ordahl, editor. *Captain John Smith*. Chapel Hill: University of North Carolina Press, 1988.

Luccketti, Nicholas. "Excavations at Bacon's Castle" in W. M. Kelso and R. Most, Editors. *Earth Patterns*. Charlottesville, VA: University Press of Virginia, 1990.

Neiman, Fraser. *The "Manner House" Before Stratford*. Stratford Hall, 1980.

Noël Hume, Ivor. *Here Lies Virginia*. Charlottesville, VA: University Press of Virginia, 1963.

    *Martin's Hundred*. New York: Knopf, 1982.

    *The Virginia Adventure*. New York: Knopf, 1994.

Outlaw, Alain Charles. *Governor's Land: Archaeology of Early Seventeenth-Century Virginia Settlements*. Charlottesville, VA: University Press of Virginia, 1990.

George Percy. [1608?] *Observations gathered out of "A Discourse of the Southern Colony in Virginia by the English, 1606."* Edited by David B. Quinn. Charlottesville, VA: University Press of Virginia, 1967.

Rountree, Helen Clark. *The Powhatan Indians of Virginia: Their Traditional Culture*. Norman: University of Oklahoma Press, 1989.

    *Pocohontas's Peoples: The Powhatan Indians of Virginia Through Four Centuries*. Norman: University of Oklahoma Press, 1990.

Reinhart, Theodore R. and Dennis J. Pogue. *The Archaeology of 17th Century Virginia*. Special Publication No. 30 of the Archaeological Society of Virginia, Richmond, 1993.

Strachey, William. [1612] *The Historie of Travell Into Virginia Britania*. Edited by Louis B. Wright and Virginia Freund. London: Hakluyt Society, 1953.

Strachey, William. "[1610] A True Reportory of the Wreck and Redemption of Sir Thomas Gates, Knight." In *A Voyage to Virginia in 1609, Two Narratives*, edited by Louis B. Wright. Charlottesville, VA: University Press of Virginia, 1964.

Yonge, Samuel H. *The Site of Old "James Towne"*. Richmond, VA: APVA, 1903.